PLEASURE STEAMERS
OF THE
YORKSHIRE COAST

PLEASURE STEAMERS
OF THE
YORKSHIRE COAST

ANDREW GLADWELL

AMBERLEY

The Yorkshire Coast provided outstanding scenery for passengers from the main resorts of Scarborough and Bridlington. Places such as Flamborough, Whitby and Robin Hood's Bay were best viewed from a pleasure steamer.

Frontispiece: The Yorkshire resorts of Scarborough and Bridlington provided pleasure steamer cruises for well over a century. Vessels such as the *Coronia* typified the type of pleasure steamers that operated services. They provided popular cruises for generations of holidaymakers.

First published 2014

Amberley Publishing
The Hill, Stroud
Gloucestershire, GL5 4EP

www.amberley-books.com

British Library Cataloguing in Publication Data.
A catalogue record for this book is available from the British Library.

ISBN 978 1 4456 1454 0
Ebook ISBN 978 1 4456 1468 7

Typeset in 10pt on 13pt Sabon.
Typesetting and Origination by Amberley Publishing.
Printed in the UK.

Contents

The Harbour & Pleasure cobles Bridlington.

The Yorkshire coastline has been an area where pleasure steamers have operated for almost 200 years. It has seen some of the most distinctive and well-loved pleasure boats provide cruises along the dramatic coastline. Popular services still exist to experience what our ancestors once enjoyed on their holidays at Scarborough or Bridlington.

Acknowledgements

This book has been written to evoke the heritage and atmosphere of the little-known pleasure steamers that have plied the Yorkshire Coast since Victorian times. In compiling this book I have been grateful for the help and co-operation of several individuals. In particular, I would like to thank Jill Harvey for allowing me to use most of the images in this book from her splendid collection. Her magnificent support for this book is appreciated. I would also like to thank Kieran McCarthy, John Higgins, Jean Spells, Mark Harrison, Tony Smith and Adam Johnson for their contribution to the project.

Websites

For further information on paddle and pleasure steamers
www.heritagesteamers.co.uk

For cruises by the vintage excursion ship *Balmoral*
www.mvbalmoral.org.uk

For cruises by the paddle steamer *Waverley*
 www.waverleyexcursions.co.uk

For details of the Paddle Steamer Preservation Society
www.paddlesteamers.org

For cruises by the paddle steamer *Kingswear Castle*
www.dartmouthrailriver.co.uk

Introduction

The Yorkshire Coast, like its Trans-Pennine rival the Lancashire Coast, witnessed a relatively short life as a thriving pleasure cruising coastline. It saw services develop during the mid-Victorian period amid an atmosphere of intense rivalry. One characteristic that stayed with the various fleets throughout the Yorkshire pleasure steamer era was that many vessels were tugs and therefore had a dual purpose. In early days, they were paddle-propelled and in later days, they were screw-driven.

Paddle steamers gained popularity on the Yorkshire Coast in the 1850s. Early paddle steamers to arrive on the coast included the *Streonshalh* at Whitby in 1836 and *Royal Victoria* at Scarborough from 1847 onwards. These were paddle tugs and lacked the fine facilities that typified later paddle steamers.

Early Yorkshire paddle steamers were frequently involved in accidents and near misses. Apart from hitting other vessels, the paddle steamers often hit rocks and without adequate safety and lifesaving equipment, accidents often resulted in the loss of steamers. The 1860s saw a great many short-lived paddle steamers in North Yorkshire service. As the frenzy to develop services gained momentum, operators reacted by acquiring and quickly placing new steamers in service. These steamers were often unsuitable for the coast and accidents were a common feature. Often, these steamers only lasted for a few months or a year at Scarborough before they were sold for service elsewhere.

By the mid-1870s, competition was becoming very fierce indeed. Rival operators used every gimmick and became very imaginative in order to gain supremacy. Some offered fishing cruises while others resorted to moonlit firework cruises.

By the 1890s like elsewhere around the UK, the fierce competition had calmed down and the typical look and size of the Yorkshire Coast paddle steamer had evolved. The coast would never see the elegant looking and highly developed paddle steamers that were found in other areas of the UK, such as the Thames and Firth of Clyde. Instead, its larger pleasure steamers would have dual roles as both pleasure steamers during the summer and as tug boats during the winter months. They would also be characterised by having spartan passenger accommodation. These paddle steamers had no large and luxurious deck houses and saloons but instead, the typical steamer used temporary awnings on open decks. Cruises would also be shorter and more local than elsewhere as the Yorkshire coastline lacked the vast number of large piers and harbours that were found elsewhere in the UK.

There would only ever be two main seaside resorts that would host a pleasure steamer tradition and both Scarborough and Bridlington tended to have steamers that were linked to each individual resort. *Cambria*, *Scarborough* and *Bilsdale* were the most famous paddle steamers that were linked with Scarborough. They provided a wide range of cruises along the Yorkshire Coast up to the mid 1930s. Bridlington had the smaller *Frenchman* as its own paddle steamer, which was frequently depicted in many hundreds of Edwardian picture postcards.

By the 1930s, times were changing and the propeller was replacing the paddle wheel as the preferred method of propulsion. The arrival of the *Coronia* at Scarborough in 1935 showed the way forward for Yorkshire Coast pleasure steamers. She was a revolutionary vessel and with her elegant lines and fine passenger accommodation, she became a hugely popular vessel from the resort.

Bridlington replaced the *Frenchman* with the propeller-driven *Yorkshireman* in the mid-1920s. The resort also had a large fleet of smaller open-decked pleasure boats that provided hugely popular short trips from the harbour.

The post-war years saw a great number of changes. Most of the older boats were sold and by the 1960s, the Yorkshire fleet was a pale reflection of its pre-war size and look. By the 1980s, the number of pleasure boats that operated from Scarborough and Bridlington could be counted on one hand. Fortunately, services were enlivened when the preserved pleasure steamers *Waverley* and *Balmoral* visited Scarborough from the early 1980s onwards. They spectacularly recreated the great days of the large Yorkshire pleasure steamers. By the twenty-first century, their visits, plus the regular services provided by boats such as the *Coronia* and *Yorkshire Belle*, meant that the tradition of seeing the splendid Yorkshire coastline from a pleasure boat survives for new generations to enjoy.

The name *Coronia* has been linked to Scarborough pleasure steamer services since the 1930s. Services from Scarborough and Bridlington have thrived into the twenty-first century.

Scarborough and Whitby's Pleasure Steamers

M.V. CORONIA.
SCARBOROUGH'S LARGEST PASSENGER VESSEL.

Scarborough had a long association with pleasure steamers. Vessels such as the *Coronia* provided cruises for generations of holidaymakers in Yorkshire from the 1930s onwards.

The first mention of boats for pleasure at Scarborough dates back to 1787 when three ships were reserved for providing pleasure trips for wealthy patrons. At the end of the eighteenth century, most passengers that could not afford one of the larger boats, hired a small boat with an oarsman to transport them around the bay or sometimes further to places such as Flamborough.

Paddle steamers made their first appearance in Yorkshire during the second decade of the nineteenth century. The first paddle steamer arrived on the River Humber in 1815 and in 1814 on the River Tyne. Less than a decade later, paddle steamers had expanded their routes and services along the east coast. One of the first Yorkshire paddle steamers was the paddle tug *Streonshalh* at Whitby in 1836. This was one of the first paddle steamers in the area. She also operated as a tug. In 1837 *Streonshalh* was towing the Whitby whaler *Phoenix* out of the harbour when the rope tore and the whaler ended up on the rocks. The Whitby whaling industry ended after this accident.

Scarborough's first paddle steamers seemed to appear around the 1840s. This was a lot later than most other resorts around the UK. One of the earliest paddle steamers at Scarborough was the *Royal Victoria*. She became a familiar visitor to Scarborough from 1847 onwards. Her master was Captain Cass who transported countless passengers from Hartlepool at a fare of four shillings. Captain Cass was described as being 'steady, attentive and sober'. *Royal Victoria* disappeared from Scarborough in 1855.

The *Transit* was the first paddle steamer to be registered at Scarborough. She was a paddle tug and had been built for service at Leith in 1848. Four years later in 1852, she transferred to Scarborough where she operated between Scarborough and Whitby, or Scarborough and Bridlington. The steamer was owned by Jeremiah Hudson and passengers paid three shillings for the cruise. If passengers wished to go ashore at Bridlington or Whitby, they had to pay an additional fee to be landed by coble. *Transit* lasted for just two seasons at Scarborough.

It was clear that Scarborough had a future as a base for paddle steamer excursions. After the departure of *Transit*, Hudson placed the *Britannia* and *Black Eagle* in service. This was clearly a show of Jeremiah Hudson's confidence in pleasure cruises and just one year later, he placed *Eclat* in service at the resort. *Eclat* was sloop-rigged and became the second pleasure steamer to be registered at Scarborough. She was 110 feet long and had a tonnage of 80 tons. *Eclat*'s maiden voyage was on 28 August 1854. This was a great success and she made a fast and comfortable trip between Scarborough and Hartlepool.

By the mid-1850s, paddle steamers were commonplace along the Yorkshire Coast. They provided many popular services during the busy summer months. This expansion of trade obviously affected the small local coble rowing boats that had carried on their ferrying work for many generations. The local coble operators all of a sudden found that big investors came along and placed a large paddle steamer in operation in competition to them. Jeremiah Hudson therefore became an enemy of the coble boat owners. They did though try and fight back by placing a steamer named *Maid of Leven* in service but this venture quickly failed.

Jeremiah Hudson sold the *Eclat* in 1855 and purchased the *Contraste* for Scarborough service. She was a bigger paddle steamer and Jeremiah showed that he was doing well with his paddle steamer service. *Contraste* had been built at South Shields and soon operated alongside the *Firefly* and the *Brothers* at Scarborough. *Contraste* sadly only operated for one season at Scarborough and was then sold for service elsewhere.

In 1857, Jeremiah Hudson purchased the *Fame* for Scarborough service. Many passengers complained about the common and dirty crew members who regularly spat all over the steamer. Others complained about the safety aspects of the steamer. Many were horrified that passengers had to disembark by means of a long vertical ladder from the paddle box to the pier. Jeremiah Hudson was fiercely proud of the *Fame* and did a great deal to promote his steamer. He reacted to protests from passengers about being seasick by stating that seasickness was beneficial to health and that it cleansed the body and rid it of disease.

The 1850s and 1860s saw a great deal of fierce competition by paddle steamer operators along the Yorkshire coast. Scarborough naturally became the main centre of paddle steamer trade as it was a highly developed seaside resort and also was more or less midway between Bridlington and Whitby. Other steamers such as *Xantho* and *Minnet* soon arrived to try and soak up the trade. Jeremiah Hudson was always fiercely proud his steamers and never missed an opportunity to promote them. It certainly was not a time when owners were modest about their steamers and it was a time of great rivalry.

By the end of the Victorian era, the *Scarborough* became the most popular Yorkshire paddle steamer. She was soon joined by others such as the *Comet* and *Cleveland*. A common feature of all steamers was the fact that they performed a dual role as both pleasure steamer and paddle tug. In 1900, *Cambria* joined the Scarborough fleet and became an instant success with holidaymakers. She had a Scarborough career of eleven years.

The outbreak of the First World War saw the withdrawal of the *Scarborough*. It was another ten years before a paddle steamer would enter service, when the *Bilsdale* plied from Scarborough for the first time in the mid-1920s. She departed from the resort ten years later thereby ending the paddle steamer tradition.

The 1930s saw a revolution in Scarborough pleasure steamer design when the *Coronia* entered service. She was a radical departure from the old dual-purpose paddle steamer. With a sleek and stylish design as well as superb passenger accommodation, she showed the future for Yorkshire pleasure steamers and was also a reflection of the Art Deco age. She was joined by the *New Royal Lady* to replace the earlier *Royal Lady* in 1938. *New Royal Lady* was a fine competitor for the *Coronia*. After requisition by the Admiralty during the Second World War, *Coronia* resumed her peacetime career in 1946 and became the vessel most associated with Scarborough in those busy post-war years. She later found competition with the *Yorkshire Lady*, *Regency Belle* and *Regal Lady*. By the 1950s, Scarborough's holiday trade was immense and all boats enjoyed the sunset of the British holiday resort. By the 1960s, things would change.

*Lighthouse and S.S. " Cambria,"
Scarborough.*

By the end of the nineteenth century, Scarborough was a hugely important harbour for paddle steamers. They were used for pleasure cruises and fishing as well as for towing and recovery. *Cambria* is seen here at Scarborough's often busy harbour.

Scarborough is the largest holiday resort on the Yorkshire coast. It is often referred to as 'The Brighton of the North'. It developed as a seaside resort when the York to Scarborough railway line was built in the mid-1840s. Very soon, large hotels were built to cater for the growing number of visitors. Naturally, trippers soon wanted to admire the growing resort as well as the nearby spectacular coastline from the sea. Paddle steamer trips quickly exploited this need and coastal cruises became a popular and essential part of any holiday at Scarborough.

Paddle steamers such as the *Cambria* were synonymous with the thriving seaside resort of Scarborough during the Edwardian era. She offered short cruises 'round the bay' as well as longer cruises to view the dramatic Yorkshire coastline.

Off Scarborough Pier.

Cambria at Scarborough. At the end of the Victorian era, the Scarborough harbour commissioners realised that it was crucial that they purchase a paddle tug that could also act as a pleasure boat. They therefore acquired *Cambria* for £2,500 in 1899. The steamer was adapted for her new role at Sunderland. She started her Scarborough career in February 1900.

Passengers waiting to embark on a paddle steamer at Scarborough. Scarborough harbour is located in the town's South Bay. This is next to the main beach used by holidaymakers and is at the foot of Scarborough Castle Hill. The first mention of a lighthouse was made in 1804. In 1914, the lighthouse was badly damaged by enemy action during the First World War.

Scarborough was a centre for fishing and its sheltered harbour became a hive of activity with fish being prepared after leaving the trawlers. In this view, you can see a paddle steamer on the opposite side of the harbour. The dual-use and similar look of many paddle steamers makes the identification of many steamers challenging.

Scarborough during its Edwardian heyday with several paddle steamers tied up in the harbour. At the start of the nineteenth century, Scarborough was one of the main shipbuilding centres on the East Coast. 209 ships were built in the town between 1775 and 1810. They had a combined tonnage of over 35,000 tons.

Cambria departing from Scarborough emitting great plumes of smoke on what may have been a special event due to the flags flying. You can appreciate the lack of deck houses in this view. Passengers had little shelter from bad weather apart from an awning that can be seen furled up in this view. She lacked most of the fine facilities in other paddle steamers around the UK.

In 1732, George II had the harbour at Scarborough enlarged. This led to Vincent Pier and East Pier being built at a cost of over £12,000. At that time, the harbour was incredibly busy with over 300 ships using it regularly. Shipbuilding was important to Scarborough at the start of the nineteenth century and at some points, over fifteen vessels a year were being launched.

Cambria's career at Scarborough coincides with the heyday of the picture postcard and so she was frequently depicted on cards. She required a great deal of work to equip her for service and she started her Scarborough career in 1900. Her career lasted until 1912.

Scarborough (foreground) and *Cambria (background)* alongside the lighthouse at Scarborough during the Victorian heyday. This photograph shows the bustle of the arrival and departure of paddle steamers. It's possible to see rows of well-dressed passengers lining every part of the deck. Cobles can also be seen in the background. These offered less-crowded and shorter trips in the bay.

The popular *Cambria* heavily-laden with Edwardian passengers wearing hats around 1908. The distinctive landmark of the Grand Hotel in the distance. The Harbour Commissioners spent over £1,650 over nine months to equip *Cambria* for her new role at Scarborough.

Scarborough grew as a spa town after natural mineral waters were discovered in the early seventeenth century. The town developed as a place to 'take the waters' very quickly and the town witnessed considerable growth during the eighteenth century. The town claimed to be England's first seaside resort.

Despite many developments, the spa at Scarborough became too small for the huge numbers of visitors that descended upon the resort in the early and mid-Victorian period. Entertainment facilities were frequently developed to cater for the ever-increasing influx of visitors.

The lighthouse stands on Vincent's Pier which was named after its engineer named William Vincent. The Lighthouse dates from the early nineteenth century and the building and tower was further developed in the mid-nineteenth century when the harbour became busier. The coming of the paddle steamer to the town meant that facilities needed to be improved.

The paddle steamer *Cambria* at Scarborough Pier. *Cambria*'s arrival at the Yorkshire resort coincided with the Edwardian boom in picture postcards which means that she is shown frequently on cards. *Cambria* performed her tug boat role well and saved many vessels.

The small and distinctive fishing village of Robin Hood's Bay was one of the scenic beauties for passengers cruising along the Yorkshire Coast. The beauty spot is situated fifteen miles north of Scarborough and five miles south of Whitby.

THE EAST CLIFF WHITBY.

Scarborough departing from Whitby. She was built by Lewis & Company of London. She made the delivery trip to Scarborough from London in just twenty-two hours. This obviously showed her great speed and it was clear from the start that she would become the biggest threat ever to the other Yorkshire paddle steamers. *Scarborough* had a distinct lack of deck houses. This was a common feature of early paddle steamers. Passengers were therefore able to enjoy the sun on sunny warm days, they were offered little protection from the elements.

Tourism developed in Whitby during Georgian times and expanded when the railways reached the town in 1839. The town has always had strong maritime and tourism links. Captain Cook learnt his seamanship skills in the town and Whitby also became an important centre for herring fishing and for whaling fleets.

Whitby faced more challenging times when ship building and ship repairing developed on a larger scale elsewhere.

Pleasure steamers were never as popular at Whitby as they were at Scarborough and Bridlington as those resorts had highly developed hotels and entertainment facilities that attracted large numbers of holidaymakers.

Camperdown at Whitby. She was built in 1868 at Greenock and was registered at Middlesbrough.

Opposite below: *Scarborough* at Whitby. Note Edwardian passengers being ferried ashore by small boats. The massive canvas awning covering the aft section of the promenade deck was to give protection from poor weather. She became synonymous with her namesake resort at the end of the nineteenth century.

She entered service along the North Yorkshire coast in 1866. She became the most famous of the early paddle steamers along the coast and had a career of forty-eight years at Scarborough.

Cambria departing from Whitby for a cruise around 1910. One of the earliest paddle steamers to call at Whitby was the *Tourist* in 1823. The paddle tug *Hilda* was owned and operated from Whitby in 1853. *Swallow* was acquired for Whitby service in 1868 by Captain Swallow. *Swallow* had originally been built as *Queen Victoria* and was in a poor condition. It therefore lasted a short while before being sold for further service at Liverpool.

Whitby Abbey is shown high above the harbour in this view. It is famous for its association with the novel *Dracula* by Bram Stocker. With its well-established historical and literary links to Captain Cook, the whaling industry and Count Dracula, Whitby has always had incredibly strong attractions for tourism. Its picturesque harbour has always been a natural magnet for daytrippers.

The North East Railway paddle steamer *Cleveland* of 1881. Yorkshire paddle steamers never gained the popularity of those around the rest of the UK. This was due to the fact that services never developed like those on the Bristol Channel or Thames because of a lack of piers that could be used. The Yorkshire steamers also never had the ample or luxurious passenger facilities that were found elsewhere.

An unknown paddle steamer at Whitby. It was possibly taken around the time of the First World War. Townsfolk can be seen watching from the quayside while a Royal Navy sailor is attending to the bridge. The crew's washing can be clearly seen under the awning towards the stern of the steamer.

P.S. " BILSDALE " AT SCARBOROUGH

Bilsdale at Scarborough with an image of her master Captain Duncan and the massive Grand Hotel in the distance. *Bilsdale* could carry up to 386 passengers and dominated the pleasure steamer business at Scarborough for many years. *Frenchman* had a similar dominance of Bridlington steamer trade.

Scarborough's *Bilsdale* was originally built as *Lord Roberts* by W. Allsup & Sons at Preston in 1900. She initially operated pleasure cruises between Great Yarmouth and Lowestoft. After service in the First World War as *Earl Roberts*, she was sold to the Furness Shipbuilding Company before being sold again for service at Scarborough.

Operators were quick to realise that passengers became very loyal to a particular steamer and would always prefer to travel again on the same steamer each year. Passenger facilities were very important but holidaymakers also liked to see the same crew and captain each year. The familiar and genial figure of a master such as Captain Duncan was a central part of a good steamer. Operators therefore used his image to promote the steamer on postcards and in sales literature.

Despite having a relatively short career at Scarborough, *Bilsdale* must rank as one of the best-loved paddle steamers of the Yorkshire Coast.

Bilsdale at Scarborough during her heyday at the resort. She arrived at Scarborough in the mid-1920s. She was a sleek and fine looking paddle steamer with wide open decks and some partially-covered accommodation at the stern.

Bilsdale was owned by the Crosthwaite Steamship Company of Middlesbrough while she operated out of Scarborough. She was one of the largest paddle steamers to operate from the resort and her popular master was Captain Duncan.

1930s passengers aboard the *Bilsdale*. Photographs showing passengers aboard the Yorkshire pleasure steamers are rare. Note the blackboards placed on the rails to give details of cruises and the navigation lamps ready to be raised up the mast.

Bilsdale had a non-compound double diagonal engine. After operating for various owners at places such as Weymouth for the well-known local firm of Cosens. *Bilsdale* was sold for further service out of Scarborough in 1925 until 17 September 1934, when she undertook her final cruise. She was later scrapped. She could carry around 400 passengers at the resort.

    Bilsdale was unlike many of the other Scarborough pleasure steamers in that she looked more like a steamer made for pleasure. She had fine lines and a particularly attractive feature was her bridge and the open decks below it. Her white colour scheme was also particularly attractive and enhanced her elegant design.

Opposite below: *Coronia* in the South Bay at Scarborough at the time when she was introduced at the resort. This view shows her graceful and attractive design. She was quite a large pleasure boat and offered a good range of quality accommodation.

    The 1930s saw great changes in the fleets of pleasure steamers around the coastline of the UK. By that time, many paddle steamers were becoming old and uneconomic and many required a lot of money spent on them to give them long lives. Most had been built in the 1890s and they lacked the passenger facilities that people wanted in the 1930s. A result of this was that many steamers were replaced with new motor or turbine vessels that typified the Art Deco style of the age as well as satisfying the more sophisticated passenger needs of the 1930s. *Coronia* was an excellent example of the new type of pleasure vessel. She became one of the most distinctive vessels of that era.

Bilsdale (*left*) is shown departing for a cruise with a full load of passengers while *Royal Lady* (*right*) is disembarking her passengers. Being owned away from Scarborough, she was somewhat alien to locals but holidaymakers were unaffected by this and enjoyed her ambience. Captain Duncan was the master most associated with the *Bilsdale* during her Scarborough career. *Bilsdale* was scrapped after the 1934 season. She had one of the happiest, longest and least eventful careers at Scarborough.

Royal Lady was very different to the *Bilsdale*. She was a large diesel pleasure steamer and offered larger and more modern accommodation than had been seen before at the Yorkshire resorts. All of this was made possible by her having more compact engines than previous vessels. *Royal Lady* was also one of the very first large coastal passenger diesel vessels in the UK. Shortly after her introduction, vessels such as the *Queen of the Channel* and *Royal Sovereign* would revolutionise services elsewhere at places such as the River Thames.

Capt. Day & Crew of "CORONIA" Scarborough. 486

Captain Day and his crew aboard the *Coronia* at Scarborough in August 1935 soon after the vessel had just entered service. This was the Silver Jubilee year of George V and the commanding figure of Captain Day sits at the centre of his crew who looked after up to 472 passengers. *Coronia* was owned by Jack Ellis and was the epitome of style on the Yorkshire Coast with her shiny highly polished ventilators, immaculate wooden decks and seaside deckchairs.

It is rare to find images that show the assembled crew of a pleasure steamer and it is interesting to see the type of crew employed and the various roles that they had on the vessel. The deck crew are wearing the traditional navy sweaters emblazoned with 'Coronia' on their chests. The lady stewards are also shown. You will also notice the ukulele and accordion players.

Coronia was requisitioned by the government in October 1939 for war boom work on the Humber. She became known as HMS *Coronia*. She undertook further wartime work in Scotland and on the Solent. *Coronia* gained fame during the Second World War when she took part in the PLUTO project that provided a pipeline for fuel under the ocean from 1942 onwards. She also followed the advance ships into France towards the end of the war and became a port tender at Boulogne. *Coronia* was released at the end of 1945 and was then refitted at Poole by Bolsons ready to take up her peacetime role at Scarborough once again in July 1946. It was hoped that her pre-war popularity would be as strong as ever.

Coronia at Scarborough's Lighthouse Pier. The first Coronia was launched on 4 May 1935 by John Ellis who was the son of her owner. Her trials were held towards the end of June after she had been fitted out. When her passenger certificate was issued, it allowed 472 passengers on a Class III certificate.

Coronia was a rival to the *Royal Lady* when she entered Scarborough service in the mid-1930s. *Coronia* was vastly superior to her competitor dur to her accommodation and speed.

Two-hour cruises were popular from Scarborough and suited the tides as well as the destinations that could be reached in the time. These generally cruised to places such as Robin Hood's Bay and Speeton Cliffs but could also provide cruises to Bridlington and Whitby. These longer cruises were good for the enthusiasts, but the ordinary daytripper preferred the more lucrative short two-hour cruises.

BOBBY FISHER – Britains favourite Accordionist – Composer of 'Strolling through the Heather' Etc. Etc.

498

A rare and atmospheric image of Bobby Fisher and his band aboard the *Coronia* at Scarborough around the mid-1930s. Bobby Fisher was a popular artiste at the time and had a hit with his song 'Strolling Through the Heather'. Accordion bands were hugely popular on pleasure steamers around the UK. The drums though may have been a problem in lively seas. Note the highly polished metal ventilators, the pristine decks and woodwork of the time.

Musicians were a central part of a cruise aboard the pleasure steamers from Scarborough and Bridlington and are often shown in deck shots.

Early in her career, *Coronia* passed the famous old Cunard ship *Mauretania* when the liner passed on her way to the scrapyard at Rosyth, Both *Coronia* and *Royal Lady* provided capacity cruises to see this emotional event.

Coronia commenced her Scarborough career in the year of George V's Silver Jubilee – 1935. The 1930s were glory days for UK pleasure boats due to the huge popularity of the seaside holiday and new developments such as the Holidays with Pay Act at the time.

The first *Coronia* had a large and comfortable saloon on the main deck and a buffet lounge with good windows to observe the passing scenery. Her engines were built by the National Gas & Oil Company of Ashton-under-Lyne.

M/V "CORONIA", SCARBOROUGH.

The first *Coronia* was built in 1935 at the Warren Shipyard at New Holland. She was 130 feet in length and had a width of 26 feet. Like many ships of her era, she had a flared hull.

"CORONIA" SCARBOROUGH'S
TWIN SCREW PASSENGER VESSEL

Coronia and *Royal Lady* would undertake popular coastal trips to Robin Hood's Bay or Filey during the inter-war years. It was usual for musicians to perform during the cruise and they played the popular tunes of the day.

Coronia at Scarborough. Jack Ellis was the first master of the first *Coronia* as well as being her owner. When he took her into Scarborough for the first time she was met with universal praise. Everybody admired her sleek lines, luxury and fine passenger accommodation. She was quite unlike the old paddle steamers of earlier decades.

She had been built at Hull at the Warren yard and was 130 feet in length. Her entry into service meant that there was strong competition between her and the *Royal Lady*. The harbour witnessed many skirmishes in the battle to get passengers. Between them, the vessels could carry almost 1,000 passengers.

The attractive white hull of the *Coronia* is seen to the full effect in this view.

The "CORONIA". Scarborough.   GRAY

Coronia had a dummy (forward) funnel fitted around 1937. Both of her funnels were painted bright red with a black top. She looked very smart in this new livery and the two funnels gave her a very pleasing appearance.

M/V. "CORONIA", SCARBOROUGH'S LUXURY PASSENGER VESSEL.

Coronia had a long and happy link with the resort of Scarborough. Many of the pleasure steamers that operated services out of Scarborough and Bridlington were often tugs and had a somewhat spartan look to them. *Coronia* had an altogether more attractive look with fine lines and plentiful covered and open passenger accommodation.

Royal Lady in front of Scarborough's famous promenade. The seafront of the South Bay is dominated by the Grand Hotel. The hotel was designed by Cuthbert Broderick and opened in 1867. At the time, it was one of the largest hotels in the world. It was designed with the theme of time. It has four towers to represent the seasons, twelve floors for the months of the year, fifty-two chimneys for the weeks, and it originally had 365 bedrooms. The hotel was designed in the shape of a 'V' in honour of Queen Victoria.

Royal Lady departing from the harbour entrance at Scarborough. *Royal Lady* and *Coronia* were hugely popular in the days before the Second World War. With a combined passenger number of nearly 1,000, they could transport large number from the Yorkshire resort on coastal cruises. At the time, most people would arrive by train or coach. A trip by pleasure boat was an integral part of their holiday.

Royal Lady at Scarborough. *Royal Lady* ended her Scarborough service in 1937. She later departed from the Yorkshire resort for new owners at Malta. Sadly, her career there would only last a few years before she was lost during the Second World War.

New Royal Lady in the South Bay at Scarborough. *New Royal Lady* arrived at Scarborough for service in 1938. This new pleasure boat was better suited to providing real opposition to the *Coronia*. It was the wrong time to place a new vessel in service as war was about to erupt.

Coronia's design was sleek and graceful and provided excellent passenger facilities for holidaymakers at the resort.

Coronia was synonymous with Scarborough and coastal pleasure cruising from the resort. She typified the 1930s and her introduction was very different to the usually quite basic facilities and look of the paddle steamers that plied from the resort from Victorian times. The introduction of new and more economic motor ships to replace elderly paddle steamers was copied elsewhere around the UK.

Bridlington's Pleasure Steamers

5201 S.S. Yorkshireman, Bridlington.

Pleasure steamer services at the popular resort of Bridlington were provided by dual-purpose tugs such as the *Frenchman* and *Yorkshireman*. Pleasure steamer services at Bridlington were always overshadowed by those at Scarborough.

Bridlington developed as a base for pleasure steamers at about the same time as its neighbour Scarborough. Bridlington's most famous paddle steamer arrived at the resort in 1899 and was named the *Frenchman*. It had the normal Yorkshire Coast dual role as both a summer season pleasure steamer and during the winter months it undertook towing and recovery work. It had been originally built as the *Coquet* in 1892 at South Shields. *Frenchman*'s design due to her role, meant that her decks lacked any deck houses or any elaborate passenger accommodation. The only protection for passengers on the deck was a frame at the stern that allowed an awning to be used in poor weather. Paddle steamers like the *Frenchman* primarily operated short cruises round the bay. Such cruises more than satisfied the needs of the typical Edwardian passenger, who saw a cruise on a paddle steamer as an integral part of a holiday at the seaside. Other paddle steamers of course visited Bridlington, such as the *Scarborough*, but it was the *Frenchman* that became a firm Bridlington favourite and was depicted on countless picture postcards during the Edwardian heyday.

Frenchman was lengthened in 1906 and continued to ply for trade in the years up to the First World War. She was requisitioned during the conflict and undertook important defence duties. She was released in 1919 and soon took up her normal peacetime role. By this time, the larger *Scarborough* had gone and she was therefore able to take up her regular cruising pattern without major opposition.

By this time, the days of the paddle steamer were numbered in Yorkshire and for a time, *Frenchman* became the only paddle steamer operating in the area. In 1925, the *Bilsdale* was introduced at Scarborough and it seemed for a while that the two paddlers would keep the tradition alive. *Frenchman* finished her Bridlington career in 1927. She had given twenty-four summers of exemplary service to the resort and had become a favourite paddle steamer to many thousands of holidaymakers.

By the 1920s and 1930s, the screw was taking over from the paddle wheel as the most popular method of propulsion. At this time, the harbour at Bridlington saw the arrival of small motor boats such as the *Girls Own* and *Britannia*. These took over from the traditional coble boats and allowed passengers to be carried faster and were less reliant on weather conditions. Boats such as the *Britannia* lacked any deck houses or bridge and provided short trips round the bay.

There was a great need though to put in service a boat that could take on longer cruises as well as taking larger numbers. The screw-driven *Yorkshireman* was therefore placed in service at Bridlington in the late 1920s. Like her predecessor, the *Frenchman*, she had a dual use as a pleasure boat and as a tug during winter months. She operated short trips round the bay as well as longer trips. She was a two class boat and had better passenger accommodation than her predecessor, although the obligatory awning was placed towards the stern for poor weather. Like *Frenchman*, *Yorkshireman* soon became a firm favourite and became firmly linked with Bridlington on countless postcards.

The inter-war years saw Bridlington at its busiest. The *Yorkshireman* was the main Bridlington pleasure boat and smaller favourites such as the *Royal Jubilee*, *Girls Own*, *Princess Marina* and *New Royal Sovereign* made up the fleet. By 1936, an impressive seven pleasure boats plied from the busy harbour. In the years that led up to the Second World War, new boats including the *Boys Own* and *Yorkshire Belle* entered service.

The Second World War inevitably affected the Bridlington pleasure boats as vessels were quickly requisitioned and they soon performed important work for the war effort. Inevitably, there would be losses and *Yorkshire Belle* and *New Royal Sovereign* never returned to their Bridlington trade.

With peace in 1945, demobbed servicemen relished the chance to return to their happy seaside holidays with their families again. This led to a great surge in popularity of the Bridlington pleasure boat fleet and new pleasure boats were introduced such as a splendid new *Yorkshire Belle* in 1947. *Thornwick* was another popular addition to the fleet. By the 1950s, things were changing and with changes such as the mass usage of the motor car and new holiday patterns, pleasure boat usage would change. Many of the boats were becoming quite old and needed a lot of repair work. 1955 sadly saw the withdrawal of the *Yorkshireman* from Bridlington. She had become firmly linked with the resort for several decades and had provided fine service to the resort. With her withdrawal, Bridlington was left with many fine but smaller pleasure boats to carry on the coastal cruising tradition.

THE HARBOUR, BRIDLINGTON.

THE HARBOUR, BRIDLINGTON

e Harbour, Bridlington.

RELIABLE SERIES. R1816

Frenchman sometimes shared Bridlington with the *Scarborough*. *Frenchman* was based at Bridlington, but *Scarborough* was based at the resort whose name she bore. *Scarborough* would usually provide trips to Bridlington and on occasions would provide short trips around the bay. She had two side-lever surface-condensing engines. Her single cylinder engines were built by Rennoldson at South Shields. They could provide a motive power of 225 indicated horse power.

Frenchman became synonymous with Bridlington during the early part of the twentieth century. The Yorkshire coast paddle steamer services were confined to providing pleasure steamer cruises along the exposed coastline. There was no need to provide a regular ferry service between the mainland and islands as there was on the Firth of Clyde. This meant that services in Yorkshire were harder to maintain as there were no regular year-round passengers. The area had to rely on the short summer season with its often challenging weather conditions.

Opposite above: In 1909, *Frenchman* provided affordable trips to Flamborough Cliffs and Speeton at sixpence a trip. The cost of a trip to Hornsea or Scarborough from Bridlington cost around one shilling in Edwardian times.

Opposite below: Postcard showing a painting of Bridlington Harbour at night.

Frenchman would undertake pleasure cruises between May and September of each year. She would offer a modest number of cruises along the coast and to other resorts as well as short trips round the bay to satisfy the Edwardian appetite for fresh sea air.

Huge plumes of black smoke are emitted from the *Frenchman* as she departs from the harbour. Note the huge crowds that line the harbour wall to see her depart. The local coble boats are also well-laden in the harbour taking passengers for a trip.

Frenchman at Bridlington. This rare close-up view shows the layout of the *Frenchman*. Her design was somewhat compact and sturdy due to her roles. Note that the gangway on the sponson used for landing passengers. Passengers frequently had their photographs taken aboard the steamers. This was the age before mass ownership of cameras and the photo taken on or close to the steamer may have been the only souvenir of a holiday.

The paddle steamer *Frenchman* in Bridlington harbour. She was built as a tug by Earle's Shipbuilding & Engineering Company at Hull in 1892 with a tonnage of 137 tons.

The *Frenchman* during her time at Bridlington. Countless postcards were produced of her at her Bridlington home during her heyday at the resort. The sheltered harbour enabled steamers such as the *Frenchman* to embark passengers easily unlike exposed iron piers elsewhere.

A fine view of the *Frenchman* during her heyday. *Frenchman* made over 100 trips from Bridlington during her first year in service at the resort. Her season usually started around May and lasted until September. She dominated Bridlington trade. Other paddle steamers such as *Cambria* made occasional visits.

Frenchman had elaborate wooden carvings at her bow, which gave her a pleasing appearance and made her more attractive to holidaymakers as she otherwise looked like a working tug boat. She had a frame in front of her bridge for an extra tarpaulin to protect passengers in poor weather. The Yorkshire steamers always had a lot of protection from the elements. Presumably, challenging weather was a permanent feature of a cruise along the Yorkshire coastline!

Frenchman had an open bridge, which meant that her master and crew would have to endure the elements. Holidaymakers would surround the master and helmsman during the cruise.

Frenchman at Bridlington. Captain George Spence was the figure most associated with the steamer as he had a fine reputation for handling her. He died suddenly in April 1925.

The harbour at Bridlington was one of the most popular attractions in the town. The arrival and departure of pleasure steamers was a popular pursuit in Edwardian times.

Frenchman departed from Bridlington for the last time after the 1927 season. She was a favourite at the resort and her departure signalled the end of the paddle steamer in the area. Her boilers and engines were removed for scrap, but her hull was used for coal storage for a time afterwards.

The Yorkshire resorts attracted crowds of trippers from the great industrial towns and cities. Most of these people never saw the sea or a river during their everyday lives, so a trip aboard a steamer was a very exciting thing to do.

The Thames Estuary and the Firth of Clyde were more succesful than Bridlington or Scarborough, because they had many places where a paddle steamer could stop for big crowds of passengers and had impressive piers which could accommodate many large steamers. Yorkshire, however, developed its own unique atmosphere and services.

The harbour at Bridlington was one of the largest and most sheltered on the East Coast. Both Bridlington and Scarborough had busy harbours with fishing as well as ships repairs taking place alongside pleasure cruises.

Frenchman had a speed of a little over ten knots. She sometimes shared the harbour at Bridlington. Between them, the steamers could carry almost 600 passengers.

Initially a paddle tug, *Frenchman* was adapted in Edwardian times by her builders to undertake excursion work. She did this during the summer months and returned to towing duties during the winter months. *Frenchman* was a hugely popular steamer with Bridlington holidaymakers.

Opposite below: *Frenchman* at Bridlington. She was strongly linked with Bridlington from 1899 onwards. She was yet another tug and was normally based at Hull, but provided pleasure cruises from Bridlington between May and September each year. Bridlington was very lucky as the steamers could operate at the very centre of the town and the excitement of a steamer arriving or departing encouraged people to rush for a cruise.

Bridlington Harbour.

While the paddle steamer era was at Bridlington, small boats known locally as 'cobles' worked at the harbour taking daytrippers for short trips around the bay.

Opposite above: *Frenchman* at Bridlington around 1908. Small fishing boats known locally as 'cobles' were often used at places such as Bridlington to offer short cruises in and around the harbour. Edwardian folk had an insatiable appetite for short cruises at Yorkshire coastal resorts and this view shows how busy things would become.

Opposite below: *Frenchman* departing for a cruise at Bridlington. In good weather her promenade deck was open for passengers to enjoy the sunshine. You can see the framework for an awning at the stern. In more challenging weather, a canvas awning was placed on top of this to offer protection to passengers.

This view of *Frenchman* at Bridlington shows the bare aft deck. Note the rolled up canvas cover linking the funnel and stern that was unrolled in poor weather. Steamers such as the *Frenchman* would often carry a musician to entertain passengers. Larger steamers such as the *Scarborough* would often have a small band.

Postcard from Bridlington, moving away slightly from their maritime attractions, and advertising their parades and gardens.

Frenchman at Bridlington. The resort was lucky in that the paddle steamers embarked and disembarked their passengers alongside the long harbour wall. This ensured that promenading Edwardian passengers would stop to see the excitement of a steamer arriving and would want a cruise as a result.

Robin Hood Bay was one of the great scenic highlights of the Yorkshire Coast for paddle and pleasure steamers. Yorkshire had a fine stretch of coastline for pleasure steamers to visit but was also exposed to the often harsh North Sea. It was also unlucky in that it had few developed holiday resorts with piers or harbours close together. This meant that pleasure steamers were mainly confined to Scarborough and Bridlington.

Frenchman had her final season at Bridlington in 1927 and was then relocated to the Humber where she provided a number of short pleasure trips the following year. After her withdrawal from service, she spent almost four decades slowly rotting and the remains were cut up in 1968 at New Holland.

A rare scene as the *Frenchman* sits in an almost empty Bridlington harbour. In busier times, competition for trade was fierce and skirmishes often broke out between operators who vied for the lucrative summer trade. Overcrowding often became a problem and owners were regularly hauled up in front of the magistrates to be fined. Some cases exist where almost double the number of allowed passengers were carried.

Frenchman at Bridlington with the shops and hotels of the bustling resort in the distance. As well as the large pleasure steamers, the harbour accommodated vast fleets of cobles and rowing boats that were popular with Edwardian holidaymakers that wanted a trip round the harbour.

While coastal trips would always be popular from Scarborough, there would always be a need to have places to visit for time ashore. Whitby and Bridlington offered the perfect destinations for a paddle steamer trip. They also provided passengers for cruises to the bustling and popular resort of Scarborough.

Frenchman at Bridlington. The paddle boxes make the steamer look very distinctive in this view. In the foreground you can see the fleet of motor boats that provided popular short cruises from Bridlington.

Bridlington opened its first hotel around 1805 and the resort quickly developed during the mid-Victorian boom. It became a particularly popular holiday spot for workers from the great industrial towns of West Yorkshire. 'Wakes Weeks' saw a huge influx of holidaymakers from the industrial towns and most would sample a boat trip as part of their holiday.

Bridlington offered some stunning scenery for pleasure cruises in the harbour. While holidaymakers could enjoy a coastal walk, the very best way to admire the splended cliffs was from the decks of a pleasure steamer.

Frenchman at Bridlington in her heyday. Steamers named *Friends*, *Transit*, *Scarborough* and *Confidence* visited Bridlington during Victorian times and did a great deal to increase the popularity of paddle steamer services. It was *Frenchman* though that was always linked with the resort.

While Bridlington had many excellent holiday attractions, passengers preferred to take a pleasure steamer trip from it rather than to it.

Postcard advertising all the nautical attractions of Bridlington, particularly the pleasure steamer *Yorkshireman*. This propeller-driven vessel replaced the elderly *Frenchman* during the late 1920s and signalled a new era for pleasure trips from the resort.

Yorkshireman was a strong link with the area that was served. It was totally different to the somewhat flowery and odd names of earlier years such as *Eclat*, *Emu* and *Hilda*. She was an excellent vessel with a good range of basic passenger accommodation as well as being able to move easily in harbours.

Yorkshireman cruising off of Flamborough Head. Cruises from Scarborough and Bridlington were mainly short cruises to view the dramatic coastline, unlike other areas of the UK, where pleasure steamer services linked a number of major resorts. Places such as Robin Hood's Bay and Flamborough were very popular attractions for passengers. *Yorkshireman* was a two-class vessel during the summer months. The First Class passengers were housed under the bridge where special screens offered passengers protection from poor weather.

Yorkshireman, like most other Yorkshire pleasure steamers, had a dual role. In the summer months she operated coastal pleasure cruises and in the winter operated as a tug on the River Humber. Towing and recovery work could be lucrative for the owners and these steamers were designed more as tugs than as pleasure boats.

Cambria disembarking passengers at Scarborough. She had been purchased for £850 by the harbour commissioners in 1899. The modest purchase price enabled the commissioners to spend time and money to equip her properly for her Scarborough role.

By the 1880s, *Scarborough* was providing regular cruises to Bridlington and Whitby during the busy summer months. Weather was often a strong challenge to paddle steamer services along the Yorkshire coast. The often lively conditions of the North Sea frequently affected business as almost all cruises travelled along the exposed coastline. There were no sheltered rivers and inlets as there were at other areas such as on the south coast and on the Firth of Clyde.

Cambria was extremely popular with her Scarborough passengers and also found similar popularity in her winter role as a tug. She made visits to Bridlington between 1900 and 1912 but is primarily remembered for her time at Scarborough.

Cambria was perhaps the most regular paddle steamer to be photographed at Scarborough. Scarborough harbour was formed from three piers built out from Castle Hill. The lighthouse was on the centre one and adjoined the Harbour Master's offices. The light was visible for thirteen miles and was shown while there was 9 feet of water in the harbour. The West Pier was mostly devoted to the fishing industry.

Cambria at Scarborough during the heyday of Scarborough's pleasure steamers.

The paddle steamer *Scarborough* was built by the Lewis yard at London in 1866 for the Gainsborough United Steam Packet Company. She became the principal paddle steamer at Scarborough and dominated trade for forty-eight years. This was a record for a Scarborough paddle steamer. The steamer was 150 feet in length and reached Scarborough in twenty-two hours on her delivery from London.

The Victorian paddle tug *Triumph* at the Lighthouse pier at Scarborough. The town was a great centre for pleasure steamer cruises as it was always such a popular holiday resort and attracted a large number of visitors. Whitby would never be able to rival Scarborough as it was a busy working port and was not concerned with tourism.

Cambria at Scarborough Pier. *Cambria* eventually ran aground at Gristhorpe in 1912. She was refloated, but was sold the following year to buyers at Hull.

A wooden-hulled paddle steamer at Scarborough. Scarborough was normally full of paddle trawlers and other paddle boats during the last two decades of the Victorian era. Paddle trawlers were very popular at Scarborough but this was not the case at Bridlington and Whitby.

Scarborough at Whitby. *Scarborough* was a familiar paddle steamer at Scarborough from 1866 until 1914. The *Scarborough* made her final cruise along the Yorkshire coast in September 1914, just a matter of weeks after the outbreak of the First World War. Paddle steamers wouldn't reappear at Scarborough for another decade.

Whitby is situated at the mouth of the River Esk and was the town where Captain James Cook learnt his seamanship skills. Its impressive harbour and abbey provided a fine backdrop for visiting paddle steamers from resorts such as Scarborough.

Frenchman was typical of the paddle steamers that dominated Yorkshire coast excursions. She lacked the size and facilities of the grand paddle steamers found elsewhere around the UK and was basically a tug that had a dual role of offering pleasure cruises. She was a fine looking paddle steamer with elaborate scroll-work and prominent paddle boxes that emphasised her motive power.

It was not uncommon in the Victorian era for unscrupulous owners to be more than a little flexible over the number of passengers that were loaded. It was indeed a period of fierce competition. One master named John Cowell appeared before the magistrates after he was found to be carrying 373 passengers when he was licensed in fact to carry just 190. For this crime, he was made to pay a fine of five shillings plus a penny for each of the excess passengers.

Frenchman in the harbour at Bridlington. Bridlington was unique in having the only large harbour between Harwich and Leith at the time when this postcard was published. It offered the opportunity for north-travelling ships to shelter in poor weather. The North Pier was 250 yards in length and the South Pier was 550 yards long.

Frenchman departing from Bridlington during the heyday of Bridlington pleasure steamers during the Edwardian era. *Frenchman* would spend the summer working at Bridlington and then returned to the Humber to work on tug duties during the winter months. Paddle tugs were low draught vessels and were ideally suited to harbours such as Bridlington.

Frenchman was involved in an accident at Flamborough in 1905. This happened when a crew member was collecting fares and had been collecting a bucket of water in an area of the steamer where there was no protection. Weighed down with over £5 of loose change, he drowned. Shortly afterwards, *Frenchman* was lengthened by over ten feet and her passenger certificate increased to 246 from Bridlington.

A moonlit view of the *Frenchman* off Bridlington. She was just over ninety feet in length with a width of nineteen feet. *Frenchman* had a speed of just over 10 knots. Initially built in 1892 by the Rennoldson yard as the *Coquet* for Mr Andrews of Newcastle, she was renamed when acquired for Bridlington service seven years after entering service.

Frenchman could carry around 246 passengers whereas *Scarborough* could carry around 300. Bridlington also welcomed the *Cambria* to its harbour on occasional cruises in Edwardian times.

Bridlington's very own paddle steamer – the *Frenchman* at the resort around 1910. During her first season at the resort she made over a hundred pleasure trips. She had a modest passenger capacity of 246 people. With a lack of deck shelters, most of these people had to brave the elements on the open deck.

A scene at the always busy harbour at Bridlington around 1904 with two paddle steamers ready to embark paddle steamers for a cruise. Some of the first paddle steamers to visit Bridlington from Scarborough were named *Transit*, *Friends* and *Confidence*. The largest paddle steamer to visit Bridlington was most probably the *Scarborough*.

Yorkshireman's post-war career was very short. By the mid-1950s, the boom in UK seaside holidays was over and the motor car and other types of holiday meant that trippers then went further afield. *Yorkshireman* completed her final season at Bridlington in 1955. After ten years service as a tug on the Humber, she was scrapped in 1965.

Yorkshireman could convey a surprisingly large number of passengers. She had two small, spartan but comfortable saloons as well as a bar that offered much-needed protection when weather was bad. *Yorkshireman* frequently hosted a musician or two to play for passengers during coastal trips. These would often play accordions.

Yorkshireman at Bridlington. By the 1930s, the propeller-driven pleasure steamer was gaining popularity. Its rise in popularity soon revolutionised services along the Yorkshire coast.

Boys Own (foreground) and *Yorkshireman (astern)* at Bridlington. *Boys Own* later became the *Flamborian*. The seaside resort of Bridlington was a hugely popular centre for short pleasure steamer cruises from its large enclosed harbour during the mid-twentieth century. The small size of the boats meant that many of them would have long careers when the heyday of the pleasure steamer was over. Unlike the large vessels of fleets such as the General Steam Navigation Company whose massive ships were uneconomic in the fast-shrinking post-war market for cruises.

Coronia during her heyday while operating cruises from Scarborough.

Bridlington had five main pleasure boats at the start of the 1950s. Demobbed servicemen and their families were keen to return to the carefree seaside holidays of pre-war days and a cruise around the bay was an integral part of this. The harbour at times became a huge mix of pleasure boats, cobles, rowing boats and speed boats.

Soon, rationing of petrol ceased and motoring started to become an option for many. Despite this and changes in holiday tastes as well as the rise of the teenager, Bridlington's holiday trade remained relatively steady during the 1950s.

Regal Lady at Scarborough. She entered Scarborough service in 1954 at the resort. She had been built at Great Yarmouth and was needed to cater for the immense market for the short pleasure boat cruises from the resort. Areas elsewhere saw services dwindle and decline. At Scarborough, the pleasure boats were a great deal smaller and therefore more economic. It was normal for queues of up to 400 people to queue at the harbour for a cruise.

The 1960s was a decade when many families were trying new types of holidays away from their traditional seaside resorts. Many people were now flying abroad for their holidays while many others had cars that offered greater flexibility. This meant that many people would now take their motor cars on holiday and would now use that mode of transport to take them to the beauty spots and local attractions rather than the inflexible pleasure boat.

Yorkshire Lady at Scarborough. *Yorkshire Lady* experienced a busy time during the 1950s. She was later taken to Eyemouth for a major overhaul where she was re-engined. During this refit she received a new wheelhouse and a different funnel. She had a speed of around 12 knots.

Yorkshire Lady arrived at Scarborough in 1951 and provided opposition for the *Coronia*. She had been built at Great Yarmouth in 1935 and provided accommodation for 250 passengers.

Waverley (*right*) and *Coronia* (*left*) at Scarborough lighthouse pier on 22 May 1982. Both *Balmoral* and *Waverley* have made occasional visits to Scarborough and the Yorkshire coast during their preservation careers.

Waverley at Scarborough on 23 May 1981. *Waverley* was built in 1947 for service on the Firth of Clyde. From 1977 onwards, she has cruised from most areas of the UK to keep alive the coastal cruising tradition. She has made several calls at Scarborough especially during the early 1980s.

Yorkshireman at Bridlington. She was the last of the distinctive tug boats that had typified Yorkshire coast services for over a century.

Yorkshireman was designed to suit the tidal and other conditions at Bridlington and became synonymous with pleasure steamer cruises from the resort for several decades. She had a low draft which both helped her to access the harbour as well as being an excellent tug for helping vessels stranded on the sand banks of the Humber.

The Harbour, Bridlington.   'Empire View.' 016·6

Passengers are seen here ready to embark upon the *Yorkshireman* at Bridlington. The harbour was a great place to spend time. It had many attractions such as the small coble fishing boats and swimming displays. This view also advertises that trippers could see the human submarine in the harbour! The 1950s did, though, see the end of the *Yorkshireman*'s relationship with the resort when she left for the Humber and a new role in 1955.

Cruises to see visiting warships that were passing the coast, or which were at anchor, were popular attractions to the usual cruise schedule. Another cruise that was popular in the past were cruises to see men collecting birds' eggs from the cliff faces. This precarious task must have been quite a sight for those on a pleasure cruise. Such a cruise today would not attract any passengers, especially as collecting bird's eggs is an illegal activity now.

Yorkshireman was built by Earle's & Company of Hull in 1928. She was owned by the United Towing Company Limited. This photograph was taken around 1930 when she was almost new.

It clearly shows the first class passenger area under the wheelhouse with its screens. A notice board has been placed on the lifeboat to give details of cruises while an officer is positioned ready to embark the quite substantial queue of passengers.

In contrast to the first class area, the second class passengers are packed like sardines in the area at the stern with the awning framework above them. They were able to get plenty of sunshine and fresh air in that position but they must have yearned for the protection and space of first class passengers at times.

Yorkshireman despite having a dual use as a tug, was an excellent pleasure boat for Bridlington. Despite not having large deck houses that were found on purpose-built pleasure steamers, she offered good passenger facilities for her limited use.

Yorkshireman cruising off Thornwick Bay at Flamborough. The coastline around Scarborough, Whitby and Bridlington offered some spectacular cruising as can be seen here. Inevitably, the exposure of the pleasure steamers to the often lively North Sea meant that many cruises could become very rough or could be cancelled.

The Harbour, Bridlington

The 1950s and 1960s witnessed many changes in holiday patters in the UK. The glory days when huge crowds queued up to board steamers such as the *Frenchman* were well and truly over at Bridlington.

The Harbour, Bridlington.

This view showing *Yorkshireman*, shows a lot of the local coble boats in the foreground that offered short trips from the harbour. Boards are also advertising trips by speed boats that became a craze in the late 1940s.

Yorkshireman at Bridlington. The departure of the *Yorkshireman* from the resort coincided with the steep decline of the UK pleasure steamer fleet.

Yorkshireman embarking passengers at the mouth of Bridlington harbour while the small *Britannia* lies close to the shore in the foreground. Several rowing boats can be seen in the harbour providing a sheltered experience for the rowers.

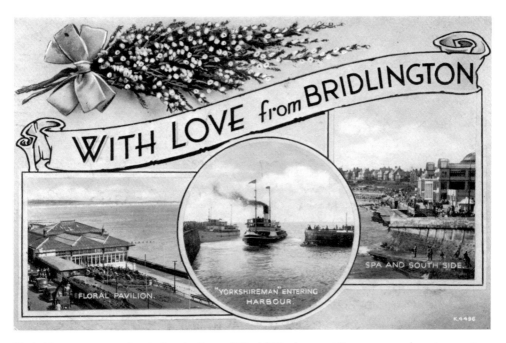

Yorkshireman saw service during the Second World War by providing rescue and towing services at the fishing port of Grimsby. After the war, she returned to take up her peacetime role at Bridlington in 1948.

Yorkshireman ceased operating as an excursion boat out of Bridlington in 1955 thereby ending a long and happy association with the resort. She continued her role as a tug after this date but was finally scrapped at Antwerp in Belgium in August 1965.

Yorkshireman had fair passenger facilities. She had two comfortable saloons including one for ladies. She also had a bar and a lounge. This was impressive for a vessel that would be utilised as a tug during winter months.

Yorkshireman was the last of the large Yorkshire pleasure steamers. Her departure from the Yorkshire coast during the 1950s signalled the end of an era that had started a century earlier.

The *Yorkshireman* (*right*) and *Royal Jubilee* (*left*) at Bridlington harbour in 1936. *Royal Jubilee* was built by Cook, Welton & Gemmell and was owned by a group of local fishermen who also operated *Britannia* and *Girls Own*. She only operated until 1938.

Royal Jubilee joined the Bridlington fleet when it was at its largest and finest. She was introduced around the time when the fleets at Bridlington and Scarborough were changing a great deal.

Yorkshireman was coal-fired and had a triple expansion engine. She was a powerful pleasure boat and was greatly admired by holidaymakers watching her arrival and departure from the harbour wall above.

Yorkshireman was the most popular pleasure steamer to be depicted on postcards showing the harbour at the resort. She spent nineteen summers operating cruises at the town between 1928 and 1955.

Boats such as the *Yorkshireman* offered popular one or two-hour trips along the Yorkshire coast where passengers could observe seagulls, cormorants and guillemots. *Yorkshireman* was coal fired and would load coal from the South Pier. She would usually board passengers from the North Pier opposite.

BRIDLINGTON'S BUSY HARBOUR. 60

Like most other areas around the UK, pleasure steamer services were dominated by the steam-paddle steamer up until the mid-1930s. By that time, many of the old and large paddle steamers were becoming uneconomic in a contracting market and the cost of upkeep was considerable. Screw-driven vessels like the *Yorkshireman* soon replaced them.

During the 1920s and 1930s, holidays at resorts such as Bridlington were hugely popular. The railway companies such as the London & North Eastern Railway produced stunning posters and other advertising material at the time to promote their services to places such as Bridlington. The harbour usually featured prominently on such posters. The attractive artwork totally evoked the attraction of a pleasure cruise on vessels such as the *Yorkshireman* and *Boys Own*.

The huge demand for pleasure cruises from Bridlington harbour meant that the fleet expanded significantly. The mid-1930s saw the *Princess Marina* and *Royal Jubilee* arrive at the resort. Both echoed a popular member of the royal family and a special event at the time. They had the usual lack of covered accommodation and provided a stark contrast to the sleek and stylish *Coronia* that entered service at Scarborough at that time. They had a crew of around six, which contrasted significantly with the very large crew that operated *Coronia*. Although they had a basic saloon, the majority of seated passenger accommodation was on wooden slatted seats.

The 1928-built *Yorkshireman* was quite a large pleasure boat and usually provided scenic trips to places such as Flamborough. The allure of the much larger resort of Scarborough was, of course, popular to a great many holidaymakers. Occasional trips were made to Scarborough, which allowed over three hours ashore. The Great Depression during the 1930s meant that for most folk, a shorter and cheaper trip was a more suitable option.

The final pre-war season of 1939 saw the *Yorkshireman* carry on business as usual despite the looming clouds of war. Many people decided to put the thought of war to the back of their minds and resorts such as Bridlington and Scarborough reported a very busy summer season. Uncertainty over whether war would take place ensured that the Bridlington boats plied for trade as long as possible and *Yorkshireman* reported a very successful season. By the end of August, the inevitable was faced and during the first few days of September, evacuees were received in the town.

Pleasure cruises were stopped on 3 September 1939. *Yorkshireman* returned to her home port of Hull shortly afterwards and soon took up important wartime duties. *Yorkshireman*, like the *Frenchman* a quarter of a century before her, would now take up a role that was far removed from the carefree, happy role performed during summer months from Bridlington harbour.

The *Yorkshireman* spent the Second World War at Grimsby on towing and rescue work. With peace, it took time to get back to normal and to resume pleasure cruises once again. *Yorkshireman* was kept very busy with towing work at Hull for many months and did not resume Bridlington service until May 1947.

Bridlington Queen departing on a cruise from the harbour at Bridlington while the *Yorkshireman* is embarking passengers. *Bridlington Queen* started life as a motor fishing vessel but later became a pleasure boat. She was 63 feet in length, had a tonnage of 23 tons and could carry up to 144 passengers.

This busy view of the harbour at Bridlington shows the popularity of the steamers, as crowds of people make their along the harbour wall to join the ship.

The United Towing Company's *Yorkshireman* was sold for scrap after being withdrawn at Bridlington after the 1954 season. She was sold for scrap to Van den Bosche & Co. and arrived at Antwerp for scrapping towed by the tug *Workman* on 4 August 1965.

"YORKSHIREMAN" ENTERING HARBOUR, BRIDLINGTON.   K.4284.

Thornwick (*left*) and *Yorkshireman* (*right*) at Bridlington around the late 1940s. *Thornwick* was built at Howdendyke in 1948 by D. E. Scarr. *Thornwick* was a large vessel at 100 feet in length and provided pleasure cruises at Bridlington until 1965.

At the end of the Second World War, demobbed servicemen initially rushed to take up the reins of the lifestyle that they had before the war and a day at the seaside was immensely popular. Soon though this changed and families started to try different types of holiday. Car ownership also became more affordable and offered greater flexibility than the coach or train. Initially though, petrol was still rationed for pleasure use and so the pleasure boats experienced something of a boom.

Yorkshireman effortlessly settled back into her Bridlington service when the war ended. She was soon joined by the arrival of the new *Yorkshire Belle* and it seemed that the post-war pleasure boat scene would be very much the same as it was before the war.

Thornwick was a large vessel and was quite similar size-wise to the *Yorkshireman*. She could carry up to 337 passengers. In later years, her hull was white but initially, it was black. Unlike many of the other Bridlington pleasure boats, she had good covered passenger accommodation that included three saloons.

In the years after the Second World War, pleasure cruises from Bridlington were mainly short trips round the bay. A small number of trips though, would go further afield to places such as Scarborough.

Yorkshireman at Bridlington. Bridlington Harbour Commission was formed by an Act of Parliament in 1697. It was formed to manage a safe and accessible harbour for fishermen as well as an area where business could flourish. By the nineteenth and twentieth centuries, the harbour had emerged as one which was centred on pleasure boating.

BOATING LAKE AND NORTH PIER, BRIDLINGTON   L 3059

The boating lake was a gentler, less crowded alternative to the pleasure steamers, and an ideal spot to watch the steamers sailing in and out of the harbour.

By the late 1990s, Bridlington had only one large pleasure boat left from an inter-war total of eight. The time after the Second World War was a period of significant change and adaption to the new needs of holidaymakers.

The busy harbour at Bridlington in post-war years. It is clear from this view that pleasure boat services and seaside holidays were initially hugely popular in the years that followed the Second World War.

At the start of the 1950s, Bridlington had *Yorkshireman*, *Yorkshire Belle*, *Thornwick*, *Britannia*, *Bridlington Queen* and *Boys Own* offering pleasure cruises from the harbour. Although the picture looked good, several of the boats were becoming older and required expensive survey work to give them longer working lives. New vessels such as the *Yorkshire Belle* were of course exempt from such problems. Her fine and fresh looks were suitably shown on a series of posters produced by British Railways in the early 1950s to attract passengers on their trains to visit the resort. No doubt, the attractive artwork attracted countless visitors to take a cruise on *Yorkshire Belle*.

The signs of change were evident when the *Yorkshireman* was withdrawn in the mid-1950s. She had performed wonderfully at Bridlington for several decades and her disappearance from the harbour signalled the end of an era.

Yorkshireman's departure did not mean that the Bridlington pleasure boat tradition was over as the fleet continued very much as it had before. Cases were recorded of overcrowding on the boats, so it appears that there was still enough trade at the resort!

By the end of the 1950s, the general gloom bought about by rationing and post-war austerity was replaced by a consumer boom. People now had more money to spend than before as well as a wide range of ways to spend it. The new world of the television showed people that they now had choices. This meant that the 1960s would see a great deal more flexibility on the part of the visitor to Bridlington.

The Harbour, Bridlington.

BDT.

Bridlington Queen at Bridlington. 'Brid' was a very popular resort in the post-war years. By the mid to late 1950s, the picture was changing.

The early 1960s started with people tending to stay at the resort for shorter periods. The once-common fortnight or weekly stay was now making way for a weekend or indeed daily visit. This meant that people had a lot to do in a shorter space of time. People were also becoming more sophisticated and many preferred indoor attractions to an often windy and wet pleasure cruise.

The early 1960s saw many of the well-loved Bridlington fleet needing major surveys and repairs. This mirrored the position elsewhere around the UK where large paddle and pleasure steamers were being withdrawn due to the same predicament.

Boys Own at Bridlington during her heyday - just look at the crowded docks! This view shows how great these little vessels were for taking huge numbers of holidaymakers on short trips from the harbour.

Boys Own arrived at the very end of the 1930s and was built at Beverley by Cook, Welton & Gemmell. She was 69 feet in length and had a width of seventeen feet. She was able to carry around 180 passengers at a standard speed of 10 knots. She was a standard design of small pleasure boat and had quite basic passenger facilities which included a bar and saloon. This view shows her enclosed wheelhouse that was built soon after she entered service. You can see the obligatory frame towards the stern for holding a tarpaulin during poor weather.

At the stern, you can see the *Thornwick* busy embarking more passengers for a sea trip.

THE HARBOUR, BRIDLINGTON

Britannia, Titlark, Princess Marina and *Boys Own* at Bridlington. Note the extensive piers and harbour landing facilities. Lots of steps can be seen which provided access to the wide selection of pleasure boats at all states of the tide.

Princess Marina became the first of the larger sea-going pleasure boats at the resort. She arrived at Bridlington in 1935 after spending several years at Great Yarmouth as the *Brit*. She spent many successful seasons at Bridlington before providing services at Whitby and later on the River Thames where she kept her name.

The small *Titlark* was built in 1936 by Bolson of Poole. She operated as *Titlark I* along with her sister *Titlark II* from Poole Quay and Bournemouth before being sold to Holiday Camp Cruisers Limited ten years later. She then spent the 1946 summer season at Bridlington and possibly then spent some time at Scarborough. *Titlark I* and *Titlark II* relocated to the Thames in 1952 and were renamed as *Okra* and *Oleander* in around 1957.

Britannia was constructed at Southend in 1923 by Hayward & Croxon. A very small vessel, she operated popular cruises from the harbour at Bridlington from the 1920s until the late 1960s. She then saw use as a boat providing recreational fishing trips before moving to Ireland for further service.

Regal Lady usually undertook lucrative short, one-hour cruises. By the late 1960s, her trade was being badly affected by foreign holidays. Inevitably, she was withdrawn from Scarborough service after the 1970 season.

By the late 1960s, Bridlington's harbour was busier with motor cruisers and yachts than with the large pleasure boats that had dominated it in Edwardian times. By the late 1980s, the *Yorkshire Belle* was the last large boat to ply from the resort.

Yorkshire Belle in the harbour at Bridlington. She was built in 1947 by Cook, Welton & Gemmell. This view shows the impressive open deck space at her bow that was very popular with passengers during fine sunny weather.

TOMMY FISHER, YORKSHIRE BELLE.

Sailing, sailing, on board the Yorkshire Belle
I'm inhaling ozone that makes me well.
I'm feeling as fit as a fiddle.
The reason is no riddle.
Sail with me and you'll agree
You feel grand on the Yorkshire Belle.

A happy reminder of summer days on the *Yorkshire Belle*. This rare image shows Tommy Fisher the accordionist aboard the vessel during her heyday, along with a poem extolling the virtues of a trip on the vessel. Live music was a key feature of the Yorkshire pleasure steamers.

Yorkshire Belle arriving at Bridlington with a full load of passengers. She was yet another product of the Cook, Welton & Gemmel yard. She was built as a replacement for the pre-war vessel of the same name that was lost during the conflict. Launched in 1947, she was 80 feet in length and had a breadth of 19 feet. She had a service speed of just over 10 knots and could carry around 207 passengers.

The view above shows her landing bridge particularly well. This was situated above the wheelhouse and gave excellent access at all states of the tide. It reached a full two decks down to the main passenger deck. She had a raised bow which made her an attractive vessel and this feature must have been admired by her passengers in good weather. This view also shows *Yorkshire Belle*'s fixed wooden seating that was placed around the perimeter of the ship with buoyant seats at the centre. Ships such as the *Yorkshire Belle* had no elaborate facilities for dining. All that they had was a small bar where modest refreshments could be obtained as well as a ladies salon. *Yorkshire Belle* started her Bridlington career in May 1947 and became an instant success with holidaymakers.

Bridlington always had a mixed boating tradition. While large pleasure boats such as the *Frenchman* or *Yorkshireman* were popular in early years, small rowing or sail-powered boats were equally popular for short trips close to the harbour. By the 1960s, the harbour looked very different.

Scarborough was able to sustain quite a large pleasure boat fleet up to the late 1960s. The glory days of the old *Bilsdale* and *Cambria* had gone, but smaller boats were still able to earn a living albeit often precariously. Pleasure boats also operated popular cruises from Bridlington.

Yorkshire Belle and *Thornwick* at Bridlington. *Thornwick* is shown in her white colour scheme. She was withdrawn from service at Bridlington in the mid-1960s and saw service elsewhere around the UK.

Bridlington and Scarborough as the main holiday resorts on the Yorkshire Coast provided a wide range of entertainments and hotels for the visitor. Pleasure steamer cruises have always been an integral part of the holiday experience along the coast since Victorian times.

Yorkshire Belle at Bridlington. The 1950s witnessed many special events. Visits by Royal Navy warships were frequent and special trips were provided to view them. The Royal Yacht *Britannia* also passed by on several occasions.

By the late 1950s and early 1960s, the Bridlington pleasure boat fleet was starting to shrink from its pre-war size. The modest size of boats such as *Yorkshire Belle* and *Bridlington Queen* ensured that services survived.

1950s and 1960s views of Bridlington harbour showed a less crowded scene to that of a few decades earlier. The seafront and harbour had changed little since Edwardian days. By the 1960s, the harbour started to be filled with recreational motor cruises.

In 1963, *Coronia*, *Yorkshire Lady* and *Royal Lady* operated their regular cruises from Scarborough while *Thornwick* operated from Bridlington. *Thornwick* also made a number of trips to Scarborough.

Both Bridlington and Scarborough maintained pleasure boat cruises in the years that followed the Second World War. Both towns boasted traditional seaside attractions for their visitors and luckily, a day trip by boat remained a popular thing to do.

In 1962, *Thornwick*, *Yorkshire Belle*, *Boys Own* and *Bridlington Queen* plied from Bridlington. They were all registered at Hull.

By the late 1960s, boat operators at Bridlington were working together to try and ensure that the dwindling trade was preserved. This included less competition and more working with competitors: pleasure boats were filled one by one, rather than having several boats waiting at the same time to be filled.

The area at the land end of the North Pier at Bridlington was close to a large number of hotels, shops and other seaside businesses. Their close proximity to the harbour ensured that pleasure boat services were well advertised. There was also a plentiful number of passengers. Note the wide set of steps leading down to the water as well as the local rowing boats that were popular with generations of Bridlington holidaymakers.

During the late 1960s, the average cost of a one-hour trip was around four shillings. By this time, the harbour was very busy and a significant number of fishing vessels and recreational motor cruisers filled the harbour at Bridlington.

By the late 1960s, the pre-war heyday of pleasure boats such as *Yorkshireman* and *Boys Own* was over. Now, holidaymakers wanted undercover entertainment offered by the Butlins holiday camp or the flexibility and warmth of the family motor.

After the withdrawal of *Yorkshireman* in the mid-1950s, Bridlington saw many changes to its pleasure boat fleet.

By the start of the 1980s, Bridlington only had the *Yorkshire Belle* and *Flamborian* left from a pre-war fleet that could be counted on two hands. A pattern was then emerging that saw over half of the resort's holidaymakers taking their main holiday abroad where they were guaranteed good weather. Short weekend breaks at places like Bridlington remained popular but often became second holidays.

Yorkshire Belle at Bridlington's North Pier. You can see the upper bridge in this view with the gangway in place. The addition of this deck, which was virtually at the top of the funnel, allowed passengers to embark when water was low at Bridlington. She could carry over 200 passengers and was very popular at the resort.

The late 1960s saw Bridlington decline as a major resort as holiday patterns changed. The traditional attractions were still popular but holidaymakers now wanted to sample them in a day or weekend rather than the immediate post-war fortnight at the resort.

THE HARBOUR, BRIDLINGTON.

By the 1960s, things had changed at Bridlington as well as for seaside resorts along the Yorkshire Coast and elsewhere. Vessels such as the *Yorkshireman* that had given exemplary service over several decades had by then been withdrawn. Bridlington would never see its pre-war popularity again, but luckily despite changes, its pleasure cruise tradition would continue albeit in a more modest form.

Pleasure steamer services along the Yorkshire Coast changed during the 1950s and 1960s. The fine tradition has continued. It has been enhanced with occasional visits by the famous pleasure steamers *Balmoral* and *Waverley* from the 1980s to the present day.

Later Years on the Yorkshire Coast

The 1960s onwards saw significant and lasting changes for pleasure steamers around the coastline of the UK. By this time, almost all of the large paddle steamers were being withdrawn and for the few vessels that remained, they were facing hard times. The Yorkshire Coast was quite lucky in that it had no vessels that were too large for the shrinking market. The modest size of the remaining boats at the resorts meant they were more economic to operate and were also in pretty good condition.

At Bridlington, the decline in the UK seaside meant that *Thornwick* ended her Bridlington service in 1965. Bridlington was no longer able to sustain a large pleasure boat fleet. An increase in harbour charges combined with higher fuel costs and people's changing tastes meant that the fleet faced a slow decline. In 1968, *Boys Own* returned to the resort with a new look and name as the *Flamborian*. The late 1960s saw the leaner Bridlington fleet adapt to changing circumstances. The fleet now consisted of *Flamborian*, *Bridlington Queen* and *Yorkshire Belle*. The pleasure boats that were withdrawn, showed an amazing ability to survive and many were sold for further use elsewhere whilst others found new lives as static vessels. The Bridlington fleet spent the 1970s adapting even further.

The larger seaside resort of Scarborough saw the *Yorkshire Lady* become *Coronia* in 1968 and she joined *Regal Lady* to carry on the tradition from the resort. By the early 1970s, just *Coronia* remained. *Coronia* changed hands at the end of the decade. Soon, the once dominant Scarborough, faced the same decline that other UK seaside resorts experienced during the 1980s. With further changes in her ownership, *Coronia* headed south for Gibraltar in the mid 1980s. The resort was now faced with the unthinkable – it now had no pleasure boat. By 1991, *Coronia*'s career at Gibraltar had ended and she returned to her old home of Scarborough where she joined the *Regal Lady*.

By the early 1980s, the Bridlington fleet had shrunk even further and it was left to *Yorkshire Belle* and *Flamborian* to carry on the tradition. Most trips were the more economic short ones but occasionally, longer special ones were made. The decade saw holiday trends intensify and the tradition of always taking a boat trip whilst on holiday had disappeared for many. Trippers now travelled to the Yorkshire resorts for a day trip by car and the tradition of spending a fortnight in one resort had ended for most.

By the 1990s, the Yorkshire fleets were elderly and required more work than ever to equip them for further service. By the 1990s, an ever-deepening increase in maritime safety regulations meant that boat owners had to adapt their vessels to comply with new safety rules as well as improving passenger accommodation to satisfy passenger needs. Changes in ownership also occurred. *Flamborian* was put up for sale in 1997. By the following year, Bridlington was left with just the *Yorkshire Belle*.

By the late 1970s, it seemed that long cruises by pleasure steamers had ended at places such as the Yorkshire Coast. The preserved pleasure steamer *Waverley* had been sold for £1 to preservationists during the mid 1970s and by the late 1970s was embarking on a programme of cruises away from her native Firth of Clyde. She visited Scarborough for the first time during the early 1980s and provided the first coastal cruises by a paddle steamer since the *Bilsdale* some fifty years earlier. She was joined by the famous pleasure steamer *Balmoral* in 1986. *Balmoral* has continued the tradition since the 1980s and has recreated some classic cruises from the past. The visits by these large ships has been infrequent and it has been left to the present day fleet to provide the hugely popular cruises from Scarborough and Bridlington that were so beloved of our forefathers. There's no better way of admiring the dramatic coast of Yorkshire than from one of these splendid pleasure boats!

Coronia at Scarborough. In the early 1960s, *Coronia* usually offered around two daytime trips a day to view Robin Hood's Bay and Speeton Cliffs. These lasted for around two hours and cost four shillings for each adult. In 1966, *Coronia*, *Yorkshire Lady* and *Regal Lady* included cruises in their timetable to see the *Neptune I* oil drilling rig and the pirate radio vessel *Radio 270*. In 1966, their season finished at the end of September.

As well as the pleasure and motor boats, Bridlington also offered extensive speed boat services from its harbour. During the 1965 season, short cruises were operated by the *Bridlington Queen* and the *Boys Own*. Seventy passengers aboard the *Bridlington Queen* enjoyed some drama on 1 August 1965 when she went six miles out to sea to rescue four people clinging to an upturned boat at Dane's Dyke at Flamborough.

The name *Coronia* was revived in 1968 when the *Yorkshire Lady* was acquired from Scarborough Cruises and given the name *Coronia*. She was smaller and more economic than the old *Coronia* but was perfectly suited to the conditions of the harbour and the coast.

Thornwick at Bridlington. She was eventually relocated to Bournemouth, where she provided services for Crosons in place of the well-known *Embassy*. She could carry over 300 passengers and provided cruises to the Isle of Wight. She was a poor vessel on this run due to her slow speed of around 10 knots, so was then renamed *Swanage Queen* and placed on the Swanage to Bournemouth ferry service. She was sold in 1970 to the Meridien Line, where she provided charter cruises from Greenwich and Westminster. Sadly, her largely enclosed deck meant she was unrecognisable from her days on the Yorkshire coast. She was then altered before being used as a house boat at Hoo Marina on the River Medway in Kent.

Britannia was a popular pleasure boat at Bridlington for a number of years.

Bridlington was lucky in that many of its visitors saw a pleasure steamer trip as an integral part of their holiday. By the 1970s, the pattern of stays had changed. This inevitably affected the profitability of the steamers. By the early 1980s, the well-loved *Bridlington Queen* was withdrawn from service.

A view of the busy harbour at Scarborough during the post-war heyday of the pleasure steamers. The Scarborough pleasure steamer trade remained hugely popular during the late 1940s and 1950s but by the mid-1960s, things were changing. In 1962, the *Regal Lady* had radar fitted and passengers were charged one shilling to have a look. *Coronia, Yorkshire Lady* and *Regal Lady* were laid up in the outer harbour at Scarborough in early 1962.

Yorkshire Belle cruising off of the Yorkshire coast. The first *Yorkshire Belle* was built at Cook, Welton & Gemmell's yard at Beverley and arrived at Bridlington in 1938. She was later lost during the Second World War. Her replacement was built in 1947 by Cook, Welton & Gemmell. She was 70 tons gross and was over 24 metres in length and could carry just over 200 passengers.

The 1970s, saw the Bridlington fleet undergo a number of changes of ownership. It also saw the *Flamborian* travel to the Humber to maintain the ferry service when the coal strike hit the operation of the three famous paddle steamers. By the 1970s, the three remaining pleasure boats, *Yorkshire Belle*, *Bridlington Queen* and *Flamborian* were marketed as the 'Bridlington Pleasure Steamers'. Between them, they carried out a variety of short and longer cruises.

By the 1980s, *Yorkshire Belle* was one of only two large pleasure boats operating at Bridlington. Most visitors to the resort now took their main holiday abroad with Bridlington and Scarborough becoming popular destinations for second holidays or weekend breaks.

The 1954-built *Regal Lady* at Scarborough. She could carry up to 220 passengers and was operated alongside the *Yorkshire Lady*. By the mid-1950s, the Scarborough fleet consisted of *Coronia*, *Yorkshire Lady* and *Regal Lady*. *Regency Belle* departed from Scarborough in 1955 for further service at Torquay.

Yorkshire Lady, *Regal Lady* and *Coronia* at Scarborough. Due to the mid-1960s slump, *Coronia* was placed for sale in 1966. She provided her last cruise from Scarborough on 24 September 1967 on a cruise to Robin Hood's Bay. She had given superb service at Scarborough over many decades but the story was not yet over as she was sold to Croson of Poole for further service at Bournemouth and Yarmouth.

The *New Royal Lady* departed from Scarborough in 1939. After the war, she operated in Scotland as *Royal Lady* before transferring to the River Thames to become *Crested Eagle*. This was for the famous General Steam Navigation Company. She then provided cruises to the London Docks as well as places such as Gravesend, Ramsgate and Southend during the 1950s.

The pleasure steamers that operated from Scarborough and Bridlington managed to have long and eventful lives in other areas of the UK after they departed from Yorkshire service.

The Scarborough favourite, *Coronia*, had perhaps the most interesting career after leaving Yorkshire. After service at Bournemouth, Poole and the Isle of Wight, she departed in 1974 for use as a ferry on the Firth of Clyde, where she transported oil rig workers. She was renamed *Queen of Scots* for this role. She found an unexpected new operational role when she took up the *Waverley*'s schedule in 1977 after the paddle steamer had been taken out of service due to an emergency. Her work at this time showed the importance of having a consort for the *Waverley* to deputise if an emergency occurred. After operating as a floating restaurant and pub, she now lies on the River Medway in Kent as a floating club house.

The bridge of the *Crested Eagle* (ex-*New Royal Lady*) photographed at Ramsgate in Kent in 1953 soon after arriving on the Thames.

By the late 1950s, *Crested Eagle* was no longer required by the company as trade had shrunk. She was then sold to new owners at Malta and became *Imperial Eagle*. In her new role, she was able to carry cars. Her life operating from Valletta continued until September 1994.

Crested Eagle in her final guise at Gozo. She survived until 1999 when she was sunk as an attraction for divers at Quawa Point at Malta. Yorkshire Coast pleasure boats had a reputation for longevity.

M.V. CORONIA

IT'S DIFFERENT!

M.V. CORONIA SAILS DAILY AROUND BAY

- SEE THE VIEWS NELSON SO OFTEN SAW
- SEE THE ROCK AS OTHER MERE MORTALS DON'T
- SEE -IF WE'RE LUCKY- DOLPHINS LIVING NATURALLY
- SEE ONE OF THE MOST HISTORIC HARBOURS AND FORTIFICATIONS IN THE WORLD

BAR AND SNACKS ON BOARD FOR YOUR PLEASURE

JOIN US AND SEE A DIFFERENT ON YOUR NEXT VISIT

 ONE OF THE WORLDS MAJOR CROSSROADS

ADULTS £ 5.00 — UNDER 14 £ 2.50

BOOK THROUGH YOUR LOCAL AGENT OR TELEPHONE: 73171
WEATHER PERMITTING

Handbill outlining cruises by the *Coronia* when she temporarily operated at Gibraltar from 1985 onwards. It was a somewhat more exotic and sunnier location than Scarborough. She offered ninety minute cruises around the bay to view the rock from a unique angle as well as allowing passengers to see the dolphins.

Scarborough's Pleasure Steamers

Cruise Along The Heritage Coast

THE LARGEST CRUISING PASSENGER VESSELS ALONG THE COAST

Cruise North to the Rugged Cliffs at Ravenscar or Smugglers Cove at Hayburn Wyke, Scalby Nabs

Cruise South to beautiful Filey Brigg, Gristhorpe Cliffs & Cayton Bay

• CLOSE VIEWS OF THE MERCHANT SHIPS ANCHORED IN THE BAY •

• ENTERTAINMENT ON ALL CRUISES •

• SAILING DAILY FROM 11.30 •

• *SPECIAL EVENING CRUISES ~ SAILING AT 8.00* •

Regal Lady & Coronia are of the few surviving ships to have taken part in the evacuation of the British troops from Dunkirk during World War 2.

FARES
Adults £1.95
Children £1.20
Children under 5 no charge

• Hot and Cold Snacks • Fully Licensed Bars •

TRY ONE OF OUR FABULOUS CRUISES WHILST IN SCARBOROUGH

Handbill for the *Coronia* and *Regal Lady* around the 1980s. Both vessels kept alive the great tradition of earlier paddle steamers to view the impressive scenery at places such as Hayburn Wyke, Scalby Nabs, Filey Brigg and Gristhorpe.

Flamborian left Bridlington in 1998 and was then acquired for further service between Poole, Brownsea and Swanage as part of the Dorset Belles fleet. She kept the name *Flamborian*. Sadly, after disagreements over where she could operate, she was withdrawn from service.

Flamborian during her days operating out of Poole. She was sold for further service in Devon in 2004. This came to nothing and she was later sold for static use.

In 1982, a buyer moved the *Queen of Scots* to the River Medway in Kent. She was refitted at Gravesend for her new role and was later renamed as *Rochester Queen*. She was later moored alongside the Rochester Bridge close to the famous Norman castle. The venture was successful for several years, but in 1993, the venture failed. In October 1994, *Rochester Queen* was moved further up the Medway to serve as a floating club-house for a yacht club. *Rochester Queen* remains in this role to this day and looks quite different from her heyday on the Yorkshire Coast at Scarborough. She is shown here at Rochester in 1985, viewed from the veteran paddle steamer *Kingswear Castle*.

The post-war pleasure boats, such as the *Yorkshire Belle*, kept alive the tradition of the *Frenchman* and *Yorkshireman* at Bridlington. Luckily, despite a mountain of threats to operating, the tradition has survived and flourishes today.

The 1947 *Waverley* began her preservation career in May 1975. In 1977, the operation faced ruin when she ran aground on the Gantock rocks on the Firth of Clyde. *Queen of Scots* (ex-*Coronia*) deputised for the *Waverley* and carried over 14,000 passengers on the Clyde thereby helping to keep the whole operation going.

Waverley was sold for £1 in 1974 by Caledonian MacBrayne to the Paddle Steamer Preservation Society. Since the late 1970s, her cruises around the coastline of the UK has gained her worldwide fame. In 2000, she received a major Heritage Lottery Fund grant to restore her to her pristine 1947 condition.

Paddle steamer *Waverley* approaching North Shields in May 1981. *Waverley* and her consort *Balmoral* provided an ambitious programme of cruises along the East Coast during the 1980s and 1990s to keep alive the pleasure cruising tradition.

WAVERLEY

LAST SEA-GOING PADDLE STEAMER IN THE WORLD

SPRINGTIME CRUISES

from Goole - Victoria Pier.

SATURDAY MAY 9 LEAVE GOOLE 10AM Arrive Back 7.30PM or 10PM.
An exciting sail down the winding River Ouse - steam under the Humber Bridge - to New Holland (5 hours ashore - trains to Cleethorpes) £3.95. Children under 16 £1.95. OR Stay Aboard and cross the river for the afternoon at Hull £5.95. Children under 16 £2.95. OR Grand Full Day Cruise steaming down the Ouse & Humber to Spurn Head and the sea £7.95. Children under 16 £3.95. Special coaches from Hull at 6PM for an early return to Goole at 7.30 OR Stay aboard WAVERLEY and steam home to Goole - arriving 10PM. CHILDREN UNDER 3 FREE ON ALL CRUISES.

SUNDAY MAY 10. LEAVE GOOLE 1.30PM Arrive Back 6PM.
Afternoon Cruise sailing amid green fields down the River Ouse and steaming under the Humber Bridge calling at New Holland Pier and Hull where special coaches meet you for the homeward drive to Goole. £4.95. Children under 16 £2.50. Children under 3 Free!

BE SURE OF YOUR TICKETS - BOOK IN ADVANCE FROM: WOODCOCK TRAVEL 15 BOOTHFERRY ROAD GOOLE: TELEPHONE 3527 - SCOT LANE DONCASTER - 18 FINKLE STREET SELBY TELEPHONE 707176 - CHURCH STREET, ROTHERHAM : TELEPHONE 65216 - CONEY STREET, YORK : TELEPHONE 21931 - ● OR BUY YOUR TICKETS ON BOARD WAVERLEY WHEN YOU SAIL●

STEAM UNDER THE NEW HUMBER BRIDGE

WAVERLEY EXCURSIONS LTD.
WAVERLEY TERMINAL GLASGOW: TELEPHONE 041 221 8152
A NON PROFIT MAKING ORGANISATION
IN ASSOCIATION WITH THE PADDLE STEAMER PRESERVATION SOCIETY

HELP TO KEEP THE WAVERLEY SAILING—COME AND JOIN THE | PADDLE STEAMER PRESERVATION SOCIETY | write to: John Beveridge, Waverley Terminal Stobcross Quay, Glasgow

All tickets are issued and all Passengers and others are carried subject to the Terms and Conditions of Waverley Excursions Limited, a copy of which is available on request at the Company's offices, or Pursers Offices. All sailings are subject to Weather, Visibility and circumstances permitting. Catering offered subject to availability.

from Scarborough - Lighthouse Pier.

More than 50 years have passed since a Paddle Steamer has sailed from Scarborough. Now the famous WAVERLEY is coming for just two cruises. Come aboard - SEE MAGNIFICENT STEAM ENGINES - gleaming brasswork - recapture the romance of the great age of steam. Enjoy the restaurant and bar that never closes - see the magnificent scenery of the Yorkshire Coast.

History - Scenery - the Power and Majesty of Steam - Sun and Sea Air - Don't Miss It - and do bring the children for a real adventure they will always remember.

WEDNESDAY MAY 13 LEAVE SCARBOROUGH 4.30PM Arrive Back 10.15PM.
A Unique Cruise-sailing along the Yorkshire Coast and steaming up the River Tees to Middlesbrough where special coaches meet you for the homeward drive along the coast road to Scarborough. £5.95. Children under 16 £2.95. SENIOR CITIZENS - ONLY £3.95.

SATURDAY MAY 16 - FAREWELL SAILING - LEAVE SCARBOROUGH 2PM Arrive Back 4.30PM
Afternoon Cruise along the Yorkshire Coast viewing the magnificent scenery of Flamborough Head. £3.95. Children under 16 £1.95. Children under 3 Free!

BE SURE OF YOUR TICKETS FOR THESE ONLY SAILINGS FROM SCARBOROUGH - BOOK IN ADVANCE AT: B & C TRAVEL SERVICES, 72 ST. THOMAS STREET, SCARBOROUGH : TELEPHONE 72138 OR BUY YOUR TICKETS ON BOARD WAVERLEY WHEN YOU SAIL.

See Magnificent STEAM ENGINES

WELCOME ABOARD — ENJOY YOURSELF........

You will be sailing aboard a real steam ship - sailing away for a day of adventure so come prepared for an exciting and happy cruise. Warm clothes, something lightweight and waterproof and you can stroll round the promenade deck and enjoy the sea breezes. Up in the bows it's bracing and exhilarating, or sit at the stern where it's calm and peaceful, and enjoy the sunshine. Down below the lounges are centrally heated on cooler days and you must go down, see the engines and the skilful engineers - warm and cosy here too. You can enjoy a drink the bar that never closes at any time during your cruise, have a meal or a coffee at the restaurant or bring a snack up on deck and share it with the seagulls. You must visit the souvenir shop - plenty of books on sale here if you get tired of the scenery - and post a postcard to all your friends and relations from WAVERLEY'S very own post box. On deck age to watch expert ship handling as WAVERLEY arrives at a pier - ropes ashore! and the bustle, pier staff and people all add to the colour and interest of a day afloat. Telegraph Bells out, lean on the rail as WAVERLEY accelerates rapidly, listen to the rhythmic, hypnotising see the giant paddle wheels turning, passing ships, glorious scenery, listen to the band. Look through the porthole

So many things to see and do on a WAVERLEY cruise, enjoy them all - and you will find it's the great life on the ocean wave.

Restaurant · Buffet · HEATED LOUNGES · B...

Handbill advertising cruises by the *Waverley* from Scarborough and Goole during 1981. The *Waverley* was the first paddle steamer to visit Scarborough for well over fifty years at that time. During that visit, she offered cruises up the Tees to Middlesbrough as well as a cruise to see the magnificent Flamborough Head.

Paddle Steamer *Waverley* with a full load of passengers at Scarborough in May 1981. The novelty of a long coastal cruise from places such as Scarborough always ensured that the cruises were well patronised. *Waverley* and *Balmoral*'s short programmes of cruises around the UK are economic due to their short length. They also ensure that piers and other facilities are well maintained for the future.

Below: Handbill advertising cruises by the *Waverley* from Scarborough and other ports on the East Coast. *Waverley* and Balmoral usually visited as part of a round Britain programme of cruises. Places such as Scarborough and Newcastle provided an excellent stopping-off point when on the way to another cruising area. Cruises from places such as Scarborough would provide much needed revenue and would make UK-wide cruising economical.

WAVERLEY SPRINGTIME CRUISES

Tyne
Blyth
Hartlepool

LAST SEA-GOING PADDLE STEAMER IN THE WORLD

For just these few days the famous Paddle Steamer WAVERLEY is sailing again from the Tyne. If you were aboard WAVERLEY during last years exciting visit we are sure you will want to come again - if you missed WAVERLEY last year - then don't miss one more chance to recapture the romance of the great age of steam. SEE MAGNIFICENT STEAM ENGINES - enjoy the restaurant and the bar that never closes.

In days past the Tyne built the Paddle Steamers that crossed the Oceans of the World - be aboard and take part in History - enjoy the sun and sea air - and you must bring the children for an adventure they will always remember.

from Newcastle - NEWCASTLE QUAY

THURSDAY MAY 20
LEAVE NEWCASTLE 9.30AM arrive back 12 noon - OR LEAVE NEWCASTLE 12.30pm arrive back 4.30pm
Morning or Afternoon Cruises steaming down River Tyne £3.95 SENIOR CITIZENS - only £2.95

FRIDAY MAY 21 - LEAVE NEWCASTLE 9.30AM arrive back 6pm
Steam down the Tyne & sail along the coast passing Tynemouth & Whitley Bay to Coquet Island £7.95
SENIOR CITIZENS - Full Cruise only £4.95

SATURDAY MAY 22 - LEAVE NEWCASTLE 8.30AM Arrive Back 10.30pm
Steam down the Tyne to North Shields - £2.95 children under 16 - £1.50. (Sail Home on Waverley or return by Public Transport) OR Stay aboard & Cruise on down the Durham Coast to Hartlepool for the afternoon ashore - £6.95 - Children under 16 - £3.50. Children under 3 Free OR Grand Full Day Cruise - River Tyne - Durham & North Yorkshire Coasts sailing past Whitby & Robin Hood's Bayto Scarborough for a visit ashore - £9.95 - children under 16 £4.95.

SUNDAY MAY 23 - LEAVE NEWCASTLE 11.15AM Arrive Back 7pm
Steam down the Tyne to South Shields £2.95 - children under 16 £1.50. Children under 3 Free. (Sail home aboard Waverley or return by Public Transport) OR Stay aboard & sail on along the Coast passing Tynemouth & Whitley Bay to Blyth for a visit ashore - £6.95 children under 16 £3.50 children under 3 Free OR Full Day Cruise - River Tyne - Northumberland Coast - Blyth & steaming on to Coquet Island £9.95 - children under 16 £4.95.

BE SURE OF YOUR TICKETS - BOOK IN ADVANCE AT TRAVELWISE, 117 Newgate Street, Newcastle telephone 323898 or 327588 - Jackson Street, Gateshead, telephone 781303 - The Forum, Wallsend, telephone 629551 - 97 Bedford Street, North Shields, telephone 576982 - 207 Whitley Road, Whitley Bay, telephone 534447 - OR BUY YOUR TICKETS ON BOARD WAVERLEY WHEN YOU SAIL.

rom Middlesborough

BE SURE OF YOUR TICKETS - BOOK IN ADVANCE AT TRAVELWISE, Cleveland Centre, Corporation Road Middlesborough - telephone 242553 OR BUY YOUR TICKETS ON BOARD WAVERLEY WHEN YOU SAIL.

MARITIME **Sail Away For A Days Adventure**

Restaurant ● Buffet ● Bars

FROM North Shields - FISH QUAY

FRIDAY MAY 21 - LEAVE NORTH SHIELDS 10.50AM arrive back 4.30pm
Day Cruise sailing along the Coast passing Tynemouth & Whitley Bay to Coquet Island £5.95
SENIOR CITIZENS - FULL CRUISE ONLY £3.95

SATURDAY MAY 22 - LEAVE NORTHSHIELDS 9.30AM - Arrive Back 9.30pm
Steam down the Durham Coast to Hartlepool for the afternoon ashore - £5.95 children under 3 Free OR Grand Full Day Cruise - River Tyne - Durham & North Yorkshire Coa steaming past Whitby & Robin Hood's Bay to Scarborough for a visit ashore £7.95 children £3.95 children under 3 free.

BE SURE OF YOUR TICKETS - BOOK IN ADVANCE AT TRAVELWISE, 97 Bedford Street, North Shiel telephone 576982 OR 207 Whitley Road, Whitley Bay, telephone 529615 - OR BUY YOUR TICKE ON BOARD WAVERLEY WHEN YOU SAIL.

FROM South Shields - MILL DAM (NEAR THE FERRY PIER)

FRIDAY MAY 21 - LEAVE SOUTH SHIELDS 10.30AM arrive back 4.50pm
Day Cruise sailing along the Coast passing Tynemouth & Whitley Bay to Coquet Island £5.9
SENIOR CITIZENS - FULL CRUISE ONLY £3.95

SUNDAY MAY 23 - LEAVE SOUTHSHIELDS 12.15PM Arrive Back 6PM
Cruise along the Coast passing Whitby to Blyth for a visit ashore £4.95 - children under children under 3 Free OR Grand Full Day Cruise along the Northumberland Coast steaming on & Coquet Island £6.95 - children under 16 - £3.50. Children under 3 Free.

FROM Hartlepool - WOOD QUAY

DON'T MISS WAVERLEY'S ONLY SAILING FROM HARTLEPOOL

SATURDAY MAY 22 - LEAVE HARTLEPOOL 12 NOON Arrive Back 7.30pm
Day Cruise along the North Yorkshire Coast passing Whitby & Robin Hood's Bay to Scarborou a visit ashore - £6.95 - Children under 16 £3.50. Children under 3 Free.

BE SURE OF YOUR TICKETS FOR WAVERLEY'S ONLY SAILING FROM HARTLEPOOL - BOOK IN ADVANCE A LEISURE & AMENITIES DEPARTMENT, CIVIC CENTRE, HARLEPOOL - telephone 66522 Ext. 247 OR BUY YOUR TICKETS ON BOARD WAVERLEY WHEN YOU SAIL.

FROM Blyth - COMMISSIONERS QUAY

DON'T MISS WAVERLEY'S ONLY SAILING FROM BLYTH

SUNDAY MAY 23 - LEAVE BLYTH 1.45PM Arrive Back 4.45pm
Afternoon Cruise steaming along the Northumberland Coast to Coquet Island - £4.95 childre £2.50 - children under 3 Free.

BE SURE OF YOUR TICKETS FOR WAVERLEY'S ONLY SAILING FROM BLYTH - BOOK IN ADVANCE FROM: WANSBECK TRAVEL, 1 Havelock Street, Blyth - telephone 5427 - OR Travelwise, The Arcade Ashington OR Bridge Street, Morpeth - OR BUY YOUR TICKETS ON BOARD WAVERLEY WHEN YOU SA

HELP TO KEEP THE WAVERLEY SAILING - COME AND JOIN THE PADDLE STEAMER PRESERVATION SOCIETY

WAVERLEY is owned and operated by non profit making organis with boards of unpaid directors and dedicated officers and Unpaid volunteers, companies and organisations continue to and this is why the WAVERLEY sails today. Your help is need come and join us in the Paddle Steamer Preservation Society

Write to John Beveridge, Waverley Terminal, Glasgow or join at WAVERLEY'S Souvenir Shop

● BOOKINGS & ENQUIRIES FOR ALL CRUISES ● PARTY BOOKINGS ● SCHOOL EDUCATIONAL CRUISES ● CONTA

WAVERLEY EXCURSIONS LTD
A NON PROFIT MAKING ORGANISATI
IN ASSOCIATION WITH THE PADDLE STEAMER PRESERVATION
WAVERLEY TERMINAL, STOBCROSS QUAY, GLASGOW - TELEPHONE:- 041 221 8152

All tickets are issued and all passengers and others are carried subject to the terms a conditions of Waverley Excursions Ltd., a copy of which is available on request from th Company's Offices or on demand from the Purser at the gangway before going on Board the Steamer. All sailings are subject to weather, visibility and circumstances permitting. Catering offered subject to availability.

The paddle steamer *Waverley* entered service on the Firth of Clyde in June 1947 and was built for the London & North-Eastern Railway. Her first few years of her preservation life were spent on the Firth of Clyde, but from 1977 onwards, she visited the rest of the UK to keep alive the paddle steamer tradition.

Her design is quite different from the paddle steamers that operated from Scarborough and Bridlington during their pleasure steamer heyday. She has extensive passenger facilities, deck houses and a restaurant. Steamers such as *Frenchman* lacked these facilities. She is now the last sea-going paddle steamer in the world.

Scotland * Lindisfarne * Evening Showboat

for 5 Days Only

The Pleasure Cruise Ship Balmoral is back for just 1 day, this year. Owned by a Registered Charity, this Big Ship is British Registered for 683 passengers. Relax in the self-service restaurant, lounges & bars - see the gleaming engine room - see magnificent coastal scenery & Islands - don't miss a great trip for all the family.

from MIDDLESBROUGH

Dawsons Wharf

LINDISFARNE & FARNE ISLANDS
SATURDAY JUNE 10 LEAVE MIDDLESBROUGH 9am back 10pm
A Magnificent Day Cruise - view the spectacular Northumberland Coast - sail 'Round the Farne Islands' & cruise to the Holy Island of Lindisfarne - see the remote Islands - seabirds - the famous Longstone Lighthouse - scene of Grace Darlings heroism in Victorian days -on this spectacular cruise £19.95.

Ideal Short Trip for Children
SATURDAY MORNING JUNE 10 LEAVE MIDDLESBRO 9am arrive Hartlepool 10am
An exciting trip for children - sail down the River Tees under the famous Transport Bridge to Hartlepool - £3.95 children £1.95. Return to Middlesbro by public - or family - transport.

from NORTH SHIELDS

Fish Quay

SUNDAY JUNE 11 LEAVE NORTH SHIELDS 10.45am back 7.30pm
View the beautiful Northumberland Coast & enjoy an afternoon visit to Amble £11.95 or a magnificent Full Day Cruise - sailing 'Round the Farne Islands' see these remote Islands - seabirds - and the famous Longstone Lighthouse - scene of Grace Darlings heroism in Victorian days £19.95

from AMBLE harbour

'ROUND THE FARNE ISLANDS'
SUNDAY JUNE 11 LEAVE AMBLE 12.30 back 4pm
View the beautiful Northumberland Coast & Sail 'Round the Farne Islands' - enjoy close-up views of these remote Islands - see the seabirds & the famous Longstone - Lighthouse - scene of Grace Darlings Heroism in Victorian days - £10.95

CHILDREN UNDER 18 HALF FARE

Waverley & Balmoral are owned by a Registered Charity

Handbill promoting cruises by the *Balmoral* from Sunderland and Hartlepool. These rare visits by the *Balmoral* have kept the coastal cruising tradition alive. Cruises were offered from Sunderland to Scarborough for time ashore. Passengers were able to enjoy the splendid coastal scenery of places such as Flamborough during the 60-mile cruise.

Balmoral was built for service between Southampton and Cowes on the Isle of Wight in 1949. She performed a role as both a ferry and excursion vessel as part of the famous Red Funnel fleet. After being withdrawn at the end of the 1960s, she saw further service on the Bristol Channel bfore being laid up in the early 1980s.

Balmoral became the popular consort of the *Waverley* in 1986. Since that time, she has been both a back-up vessel to the *Waverley* and has travelled extensively around the coastline of the UK to keep alive the tradition of coastal cruising. Her popularity, flexibility and fine appearance have gained her countless fans around the UK.

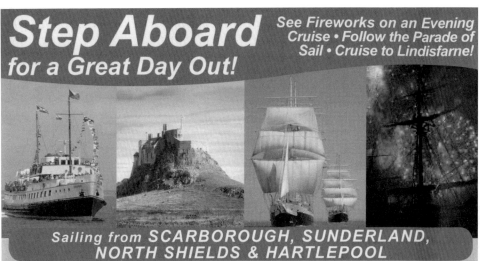

Step Aboard for a Great Day Out!

See Fireworks on an Evening Cruise • Follow the Parade of Sail • Cruise to Lindisfarne!

Sailing from SCARBOROUGH, SUNDERLAND, NORTH SHIELDS & HARTLEPOOL

*Don't miss the chance to sail aboard the Classic Cruise Ship Balmoral from a port near you! Beat the traffic and travel in style to **Visit the Tall Ships Event** in Hartlepool. Soak up the carnival atmosphere – there is something for all the family to enjoy! See spectacular Tall Ships – and much more! On board Balmoral you can relax on the sun decks, enjoy a meal or a drink in the restaurant or restored period lounge bars and visit the souvenir shop. Balmoral is owned by a Charity & British Registered for 683 passengers. There are special fares for Children and Senior Citizens so BOOK NOW and enjoy a great trip for the whole family!*

Sailing from HARTLEPOOL Fish Quay
Cruise DURHAM HERITAGE COAST

SATURDAY AUGUST 7	SUNDAY AUGUST 8	MONDAY AUGUST 9
Leave 2pm back 4pm	Leave 1pm back 3pm Leave 3pm back 5pm	Leave 2pm back 4pm Leave 4pm back 7.30pm

Afternoon cruise along the Durham Heritage coast, once home to a rich industrial past, now reclaimed and restored! Adults £15 Children £7.50

FIREWORKS CRUISE

MONDAY AUGUST 9 Leave 7.30pm back 10pm
Cruise along the Durham Heritage coast then get grandstand views of Fireworks in Hartlepool. Restaurant and Lounge Bars open all evening £17.95 *Bring friends along for a great night out - Groups of 6 or more only £16.20!*

PARADE of SAIL

TUESDAY AUGUST 10 Leave 11.30am back 5pm
Don't miss the chance to escort the Tall Ships Parade of Sail as this Flotilla of magnificent ships leaves Hartlepool. Follow them out to sea in full sail - Don't forget your camera! Limited Availability so BOOK NOW for this Great Day £75!

FARNE ISLANDS & LINDISFARNE

WEDNESDAY AUGUST 11 Leave 10am back 9pm
Grand Day Cruise to 'one of the world's most enchanting places'. Sail up the coast and visit Sunderland or North Shields £19 SENIOR CITIZENS £17. Or stay aboard for the magnificent cruise round the Farne Islands – see Coquet Island and Dunstanburgh Castle -spot the seabirds and lighthouse and sail to Holy Island for grandstand views of Lindisfarne £37 SC £35

Book Online at www.waverleyexcursions.co.uk

Handbill for cruises by the *Balmoral* from Scarborough, Hartlepool and North East reports around 2010. The *Balmoral* had been built for Isle of Wight service and was acquired to be the consort of the famous *Waverley* in 1986. Since then, she has operated in support of *Waverley* and has helped keep pleasure steamer cruises going around the UK, including places such as Scarborough.

Pleasure steamers have now operated along the Yorkshire coastline for almost 200 years. Yorkshire developed a popular pleasure steamer tradition that has endured changing tastes and the development of new technology. The smaller vessels have always been the most popular ones since the introduction of the *Coronia* in the mid-1930s.

The *Waverley* and *Balmoral*.

For details of pleasure cruises around the coastline of the UK see;

www.mvbalmoral.org.uk
www.waverleyexcursions.co.uk

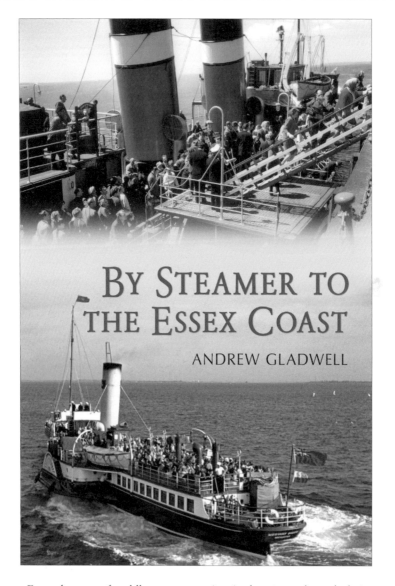

BY STEAMER TO
THE ESSEX COAST

ANDREW GLADWELL

From the start of paddle steamer services in the 1820s, through their
1930s heyday to the collapse following the Second World War and the
nostalgic service now provided by *Balmoral* and *Waverley*, Andrew
Gladwell explores this simple pleasure which brought so much joy.

978 1 4456 0376 6
128 b&w pages, plus 16 pages of colour.

Available from all good bookshops or order direct
from our website www.amberleybooks.com

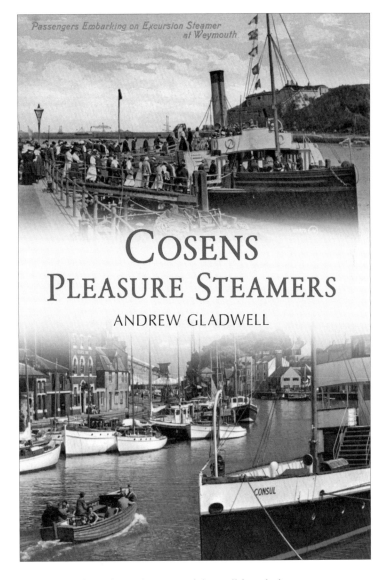

Passengers Embarking on Excursion Steamer at Weymouth

COSENS
PLEASURE STEAMERS
ANDREW GLADWELL

CONSUL

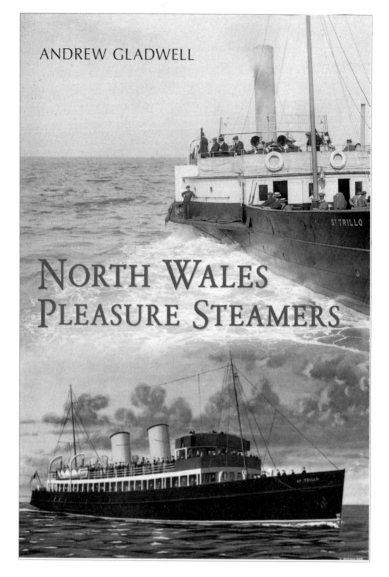